The Autism Ambassadors Handbook

The Autism Ambassadors Handbook

Peer Support for Learning, Growth, and Success

Zak Kukoff

CORWIN
A SAGE Company

CORWIN
A SAGE Company

FOR INFORMATION:

Corwin
A SAGE Company
2455 Teller Road
Thousand Oaks, California 91320
(800) 233-9936
www.corwin.com

SAGE Publications Ltd.
1 Oliver's Yard
55 City Road
London EC1Y 1SP
United Kingdom

SAGE Publications India Pvt. Ltd.
B 1/I 1 Mohan Cooperative Industrial Area
Mathura Road, New Delhi 110 044
India

SAGE Publications Asia-Pacific Pte. Ltd.
3 Church Street
#10-04 Samsung Hub
Singapore 049483

Printed in the United States of America.

A catalog record of this book is available from the Library of Congress.

ISBN 978-1-4522-3525-7

Acquisitions Editor: Jessica Allan
Associate Editor: Julie Nemer
Editorial Assistant: Heidi Arndt
Production Editor: Amy Schroller
Copy Editor: Cate Huisman
Typesetter: C&M Digitals (P) Ltd.
Proofreader: Susan Schon
Indexer: Sylvia Coates
Cover Designer: Candice Harman
Permissions Editor: Karen Ehrmann

This book is printed on acid-free paper.

SUSTAINABLE FORESTRY INITIATIVE
Certified Chain of Custody
Promoting Sustainable Forestry
www.sfiprogram.org
SFI-01268

SFI label applies to text stock

13 14 15 16 17 10 9 8 7 6 5 4 3 2 1

Contents

Foreword

Even before Leo Kanner wrote his seminal description of the 11 children experiencing *autistic aloneness* in his Baltimore clinic in 1943, parents and professionals had been searching for ways to help improve the lives of children with autism and integrate these youngsters into the mainstream wherever possible. Although the historical scientific literature describing treatment approaches for children with autism is long and varied with a fair amount of controversy, there appears to be some consensus about what works: consistent behavioral interventions that involve socially valid methods that are designed to work during training as well as when the training programs are formally ended. Typically these methods include modeling and reinforcing socially appropriate behavior with an eye toward mainstreaming children with autism into the world of their typical peers. This is the beauty and elegance of Zak Kukoff's Autism Ambassadors program.

I first became acquainted with Zak and Autism Ambassadors shortly after Zak developed the program as he was looking for professional guidance in creating each of the modules contained in this book. As a practicing psychologist and an associate professor of psychology at California State University, Northridge, I teach applied courses in the clinical and behavioral clinical psychology graduate programs. Consequently, my clinical and academic interests were piqued by what Zak had developed thus far. I was familiar with scientific studies on the use of peer tutoring to develop and maintain social skills in children with autism and knew that other psychologists have found this to be a highly effective technique with elementary, middle, and high school students. Since Zak and I exchanged our first e-mails back in early 2010, I have been excited by the groups of modules that Zak has created and has sent to me for my review and input. Zak's highly structured set of behavioral prescriptions for trained typical adolescents to follow enhances the lives of their peers with autism and the lives of the peer tutors who are trained in the program.

Zak's curriculum is loosely based on the principles of applied behavior analysis (ABA), which uses the theory of behaviorism to modify human behaviors as part of an educational process. Tasks are broken down into "discrete trials" that allow observers (in this case the Ambassadors) to break down optimal behaviors into simple steps for students with autism; ultimately, the student learns, by repetition, how to change undesirable behavior into socially acceptable behavior. Following in the literature of peer tutoring, Zak has established the Autism Ambassadors program as a specific social skills training program that is inclusive and socially valid and that builds in the sense of generalization—the notion that skills acquired as part of the peer tutoring program will be used outside of the peer tutoring program and can be applied in social circumstances anywhere. Within the Autism Ambassadors program, typical peers model socially appropriate behavior; the peers with autism learn to imitate and practice the socially appropriate behavior with the Autism Ambassador, and then these peers with autism have the opportunity use the same behaviors outside of the context of their interactions with the Autism Ambassador. Zak—as a 17-year-old high school student—was well aware of the many situations that adolescents face in the context of their school setting, and he developed roughly 40 modules to match many of the difficult areas that adolescents typically negotiate. Using Zak's curriculum, children with autism can be taught to navigate field trips, share interests in music and books, make new friends, join clubs, and engage in playground activities, as well as explain their diagnosis to peers in a socially appropriate and sensitive manner. Zak's curriculum includes clear behavioral descriptions of what the peer tutor should say or do and also provides opportunities for teaching moments for the peer with autism beyond the basic text of the prescribed interactions. The curriculum itself is a concise, teachable, and highly relevant set of behavioral interventions.

Even with good behavioral intervention programs in place, rates of new diagnoses of autism have skyrocketed over the past few decades. Early estimates as far back as the 1970s put the prevalence rates of autism at around 4 in 10,000 children, whereas recent estimates put this prevalence rate now at approximately 1 in 100 children. I have heard the word *epidemic* bandied about more times than I can count, but I am not sure if even that word sufficiently describes what has happened as of late. Resources are being taxed at every turn, skilled interventionists needed to work with these children are at a premium, and state mental health agencies are struggling to keep up with the demand for services, as children are more and more frequently being diagnosed with this devastating psychological disorder. Empirical studies suggest that intensive, frequent, applied behavioral interventions administered early in the developmental trajectory of children with autism produce the best prognoses for these youngsters.

I am happy to say that if there is a silver lining in this looming cloud, it is Autism Ambassadors. Zak's program is a phenomenal adjunct to these behavioral interventions, in that Zak's curriculum targets those youth with this disorder in the setting where they spend the majority of their daytime hours: their schools. In addition, the involvement of typical peers in the intervention program adds the advantage of both mainstreaming the children with autism in a classroom setting with these typical peers while simultaneously promoting the development of social skills for children with autism—an area that is a core deficit in children with autism. For the student Ambassador and the peers who are introduced to the children with autism in this curriculum, Zak's program also serves the much-needed goal of teaching sensitivity to the remarkable diversity of children in a setting where often, unfortunately, being different means being teased or bullied. As this next generation comes of age with a staggering percentage of its population struggling with this disorder, they might now also have the opportunity to be cognizant of, and sensitive to, the special needs of that segment of the population.

What is ultimately so remarkable about Zak's program is that he has identified a population of students in need and has developed a program with the goal of promulgating it through school systems as an easy-to-implement set of lessons. This curriculum can be used as an adjunct to existing ABA intervention programs that are school based or in the private sector. Indeed, special education programs may opt to include some of the Autism Ambassador curriculum and use it as a jumping off point for further programs that monitor treatment progress. Zak's Autism Ambassadors program represents an extensive work of applied psychological techniques destined to move beyond collecting dust on a bookshelf in the ivory towers of academia into the real world of applied psychology. The goal of this curriculum is to be used—immediately—with children most in need of social support and guidance. The fact that this program has been developed by a brilliant 17-year old social entrepreneur with a goal of making the world a better place for all children is a mere sidelight.

To the program specialists and special educators considering this curriculum, I strongly urge you to try out some of the modules with the students entrusted to your care. To researchers, trainees, and graduate students studying behavioral approaches in working with children with autism, I challenge you to include Zak's modules as part of your research or training programs. To the parents of children with autism, I encourage you to recommend this program to your school districts. To the children with autism seeking friends, I hope that this curriculum gets you on your way to more rewarding peer interactions. I know that Zak would love to hear about all of your successes and struggles with this remarkable curriculum, and I wish you success in your professional endeavors with the Autism Ambassadors program.

Gary S. Katz, PhD
Associate Professor of Psychology
California State University, Northridge

Preface

On a Tuesday afternoon at the end of study hall at Springfield High School, a high school sophomore named Justin is seated in a corner alone, busily turning the pages of a large history book taken from the shelf next to him. As a bell sounds, the class begins to gather their things and exit the room. Justin is still captivated by the book. A student aide walks over to Justin and encourages him to head to his next class. The aide notices that Justin is not reading the book at all; he is merely flipping the pages—10 pages to the right, 10 pages to the left. The aide touches Justin's shoulder to get his attention. Suddenly, Justin throws the book to the floor and screams, "NO!!!!"

Every day, thousands of students struggle to stay afloat at school. Bullied, tormented, and ostracized, they wade through a sea of apathetic—and, in many cases, downright antagonistic—faces, some of which are on individuals who might want to help but just don't know how, or where to begin. At first glance, these struggling students might look just like any other awkward kids destined to be on the outside looking in, as so many adults painfully remember being the case with their years in school from kindergarten through senior year. But these kids have something those adults never had: autism. And their experiences will, in all likelihood, be nothing like the ones that the aforementioned adults had all those years ago.

As you might have figured out by now, Justin, whose experience is recounted above, is not a typical student who is simply having a bad day. He is one of countless students struggling with autism, a very complicated developmental disorder that makes normal, day-to-day activities and social interactions very difficult. Autism is the most severe disorder on the autism spectrum, which includes other disorders with similar and typically less-severe symptoms. Justin's behavior in study hall is representative of just a few of the many possible signs of autism and autism spectrum disorder (ASD).

Estimates vary, but every year, anywhere from 1 out of 500 children to 1 out of every 64 children is diagnosed with an ASD. Regardless of the actual numbers, autism and ASDs are widely regarded as common disorders with which most educators and school administrators will have direct contact throughout the course of their careers. In fact, you may be well acquainted with someone who has an ASD, and you might not even realize it. Here's an interesting exercise: First, find out how many students are in your school. Then, using a calculator, divide that number by 64. When you get the answer, round it up to the nearest whole number. That number is approximately how many classmates of yours very well might have an ASD.

Surprised? These people will go through life feeling rejected and alone, unless we can make a drastic change, and with that drastic change, instead of the experience outlined above, these people will likely experience something along the lines of the following scenario:

On a Tuesday afternoon at the end of study hall at Springfield High School, a high school sophomore named Michael is seated in a corner with his new friend, Justin. Michael has picked out an atlas for him and Justin to read, because he knows Justin is interested in state capitals. Michael points out to Justin that the atlas also mentions every state bird and flower as well. The bell rings, and Michael asks, "Justin, what does the bell mean?" Justin replies, "That means it's time for the next class." Justin and Michael pack their belongings and leave the room.

Michael is a member of Autism Ambassadors, a peer leadership organization that aims to help students on the autism spectrum feel socially connected and fully integrated in their academic environments. As an Autism Ambassador, Michael helps Justin gain a better understanding of the logistical ins and outs of how to act, not only during a typical day at school, but during various extracurricular and school-related activities as well. It is my goal to train as many students like Michael as I can, so they can help as many students like Justin as possible.

MY RATIONALE

I began to develop Autism Ambassadors in the summer of 2008, but the idea had been a passion of mine long before I officially created the organization. Like many passions, Autism Ambassadors came from a personal experience; when I was four years old, a family member of mine (I'll call her "Sara") who had been diagnosed with autism came to live with my family. Although I was quite young at the time, I was nonetheless well aware of how she was mistreated by her peers. I wanted to do something about it, but I had no idea what; it seemed like everyone around me was either barely tolerant of or flat-out put off by her behavior (more on that later). As my typical sister and I watched, Sara was quickly transformed from a new member of the community into a pariah. Whenever she would come to visit, my sister and I wanted to include her in our games with the neighborhood kids, but we soon found that their patience grew thinner and thinner with every social cue Sara missed. My sister and I tried to explain to Sara how her behavior—the constant flapping of her hands, the rocking back and forth on her feet, the occasional shrieks followed by her clamping down on her ears and squeezing her eyes shut—were alienating the other kids, but Sara didn't seem to register our concerns. As I got older, I realized that it wasn't that Sara didn't care, but rather that she didn't know how to care. And in turn, others didn't know how to care about her.

So I took the time to get to know Sara myself, and the more I got to know her, the more I discovered an amazing person lurking underneath a veneer of cold-seeming, repetitive, robotic behavior. After several years of getting to understand her, I felt that I could act as an ambassador in the truest sense of the word, helping both sides—typical kids as well as those with ASD—understand each other.

Sara's story, I'm thrilled to say, had a happy ending. My mother, a behavioral psychologist with a background in ABA (the approach to treating autism that has met with the greatest success and the foundation of Autism Ambassadors' curriculum), worked extensively with Sara until she was indistinguishable from her peers. At the time of this book's publication, Sara is not only in a mainstream classroom with her peers, but is also a GATE (gifted and talented education program) student who is thriving socially as well. However, my experience led me to decide that I had to do something about what Sara went through—for her sake, for sure, but also for the sake of hundreds, thousands, and, as I would soon find out, hundreds of thousands, even millions, of other Saras out there.

I was determined to get my hands on anything and everything I could about autism. What I found was daunting: I quickly discovered that there was a startling lack of information about autism and that many people were confused and even intimidated by a diagnosis they didn't fully understand. And this was just the adults; any kids trying to understand more about autism, which the latest statistics had pegged as afflicting one out of every 150 babies born, would no doubt become discouraged and give up. After all, when you're a kid, the easiest thing to do is to fit in; why would anyone want to draw extra attention to themselves, especially by spending spare time with kids who sometimes flap their hands in the hallway, show little to no interest in basic social decorum, and sometimes sound like they just stepped off a spaceship when they speak?

As daunted as I was, I didn't let any of that stop me. My research concerned a family member, and one thing my mother has always emphasized is that you don't give up on family. I began seeing every kid with autism out there as being part of someone else's family, not just as some strange kid who couldn't abide by the social norms. Little by little, slowly but surely, a strange thing happened: I developed empathy. Empathy is different from sympathy, which pretty much anyone can have; we can feel sorry for people without ever walking the proverbial mile in their shoes. But to feel empathy, which involves understanding to the point of feeling what someone is experiencing? Well, that's something quite different. And that distinction between sympathy and empathy, that became the basis of Autism Ambassadors—the program whose curriculum and philosophy you will read about in the following pages.

ABOUT AUTISM AMBASSADORS

With the help of a psychologist, I created Autism Ambassadors so that others could benefit from the remarkable experience I'd had and learn to better interact with their peers with ASD. Autism Ambassadors is a completely unique approach to assisting students with ASD. Instead of requiring help from an outside therapist, or even a school aide, Autism Ambassadors relies on kind, patient, and ambitious students like you and me to help ASD students succeed in social and academic environments. A therapist might discuss popular topics of conversation with a student with autism, in the hopes that the student will then be able to bring them up in social situations at school. But with all due respect to these licensed professionals, being cool in school or at a dance is not something most therapists—or, for that matter, even most parents—can help someone with. We think students can do a better job of it, and we've designed a roadmap that teaches them how.

As Autism Ambassadors, typical students work with their ASD partners on learning a variety of normal school activities. Autism Ambassadors' modules are designed to break down various school activities—such as forming groups—into a step-by-step process that the ASD student can understand, and to help that student be flexible when maintaining perfect structural order is not possible. We'll start you out with a very simple module in the first section of the curriculum—**Pay Attention/Calm Hands**—that is aimed at younger students but can be quite useful for students of all ages. Each lesson plan in this book describes a different learning opportunity, geared toward teaching students with autism how better to integrate themselves into their social and academic environments. Lesson plans are also presented in a manner that is compatible with the distinct learning styles of students with ASD, the majority of whom tend to work best in highly structured, organized environments.

Although teachers do their best to run a tight ship in their classrooms, we all know that things can get out of hand from time to time. For instance, when a teacher says something like "Okay class, get into groups of four," what typically happens next is that the students turn their desk or chairs to join others, or perhaps get up to join their friends on the other side of the room. After a while, the teacher calls the class to order so everyone can begin the group activity. Most students probably do not have much trouble with this sort of task. Maybe those students that are shy or that don't know anyone in the class get nervous about working with new people, but most students have been in these situations and have sufficient inner resources with which to adapt.

Now imagine what it would be like to form groups for a student with ASD:

> *The time is 11:05 a.m. Five minutes and 30 seconds ago, you sat down in your chair. Three minutes ago, you finished lining up your notebook and pencil on your desk. The teacher says something, but you don't catch it because you are focused on making sure the pencil doesn't roll down the slant of the desk. Suddenly, you hear desks banging loudly on the linoleum floor. The desks start turning in randomly different directions, and this bothers you; you do not want to move your desk because it is now finally parallel with the window, and you would have to reorganize your notebook and pencil accordingly. Now you're the only one whose desk is facing forward and the only one who is not in a group. The teacher patiently asks a group nearby to come over and join you. More banging desks. Now four people are circled around you and seem to be saying loud things about you. You don't understand why they seem angry, but even worse, now you're in a group of five. The teacher said to form groups of four, but you're in a group of five. Five is too many; it should be four. This is not right. Your pencil rolls off the desk and lands on the floor. Nothing is right! Now you're angry, too!*

Just like Justin's experience in study hall, this is another scenario in which a student with ASD can be helped by an Autism Ambassador.

WHO IS THIS BOOK FOR?

Now that you know a bit about us—and you'll learn a great deal more in the ensuing pages—let's find out more about you. If you're reading this book in the first place, chances are you're the kind of person who wants to make a difference. Perhaps you're already involved in a community service program, or perhaps you're already active in your school's student government, or maybe you decided to give this book a chance because it's a topic that's interesting to you. Perhaps you're a teacher, or school administrator, whose already overcrowded classroom or school now features an influx of students with ASDs, or a parent who is friends with the parent of an Ambassador. Autism Ambassadors works because of people like you who are extremely motivated to make a change in the lives of others around them. Even if none of that describes you, don't worry; we'll give you the tools you need to make a difference. Autism Ambassadors can help you directly, no matter if you're a student, school administrator, teacher, or parent of a student with autism.

FOR STUDENTS: Let's be honest: school can be a difficult time for many of us. Middle and high school can be especially tough. A lucky few will enjoy every moment of it and will look back on these times as the best of their lives, but for many others, it will be a confusing mélange of frustration and insecurity peppered with intermittent bursts of fun and extracurricular participation. I won't turn this into a discussion about how to make the most out of your school years, and by no means do I claim to be an expert on the topic. What I will tell you, though, is how you can dramatically change the life of one of your classmates like Justin. In addition to the struggles associated with autism and ASD, Justin faces the same challenges we all deal with every day, including what must be the most difficult challenge of all: simply fitting in. I understand that you very well may be caught in that gray area that defines most high school experiences: You may not want to be the most easily identifiable kid on campus, but you probably don't want to blend in so much that you're just like everyone else. It is important to be your own person, but it is also important that your unique personality be accepted by at least a few others. These people who we come to call friends help build our confidence as we continue to face new challenges.

Autism Ambassadors gives ASD students a learning experience that would simply not be possible without the ambition and patience of a thoughtful peer. To the students who are reading this book, you should know that because we are students ourselves, we have a unique opportunity to relate to our ASD peers in a way that no teacher, student aide, therapist, or even parent can. The simple fact that you are student will enable you to establish a trust and comfort level with your ASD peers and will, in turn, help them feel more comfortable interacting with other students. Add that to what you can learn from the modules described in this book and we are pretty sure that you will be ready to make a significant difference. And who knows? Maybe that difference will have a positive impact on you as well.

FOR SCHOOL ADMINISTRATORS AND TEACHERS: The rising number of students with autism in our educational system presents a series of challenges for educational professionals, who must now address everything from a strain on their schools' financial resources to a variety of new behavioral and educational considerations. Widespread budget cutbacks are causing an increase in classroom sizes, while at the same time reducing the number of aides trained to address the needs of students with autism. As a result, teachers, most of whom have little experience with ASDs, frequently take time away from their lesson plans to tend to behavioral and/or learning-related issues pertaining to these students. School administrators, who are doing all they can just to maintain state-mandated standards while keeping the dropout rate as low as possible, now must address a group of students for whom the existing educational and social structures are simply insufficient. Autism Ambassadors aims to take some of the brunt off these professionals by providing a trained workforce, free of charge, whose job it is to help students with autism not only function, but thrive in their classrooms, cafeterias, and extracurricular groups.

FOR PARENTS: Maybe you heard of our program from a teacher, or read an article, or perhaps you even heard about it from a fellow parent of a child with an ASD. As a parent, there is a very important place in Autism Ambassadors for you, for as important as the school environment is, the school day typically ends somewhere between 2:30 and 3:30 p.m., at which point students return to their home environments. The better an understanding parents have of our programs, the more they can incorporate those programs into the student's everyday routine: afterschool homework, sports, and clubs, as well as dinnertime and family time. We encourage parents to read this book from cover to cover, make notes, and perhaps even improvise variations on our existing programs to fit the needs of their individual children. In addition to being what we hope will be an important school-based resource, Autism Ambassadors can also be a valuable resource to the community, allowing parents of Ambassadors—as well as parents of students with autism—to share their thoughts and observations about the program. We value your input and want you to be as integral a part of our program as you can.

Publisher's Acknowledgments

Corwin gratefully acknowledges the contributions of the following reviewers:

Anne Beveridge
Junior School Assistant Head/ PYP Coordinator
Branksome Hall Asia
Seoul, Korea

Kate Boone
Case Manager
MHMRA Harris County
Houston, TX

Cynthia Herr
Faculty
Department of Special Education and Clinical Sciences
University of Oregon
Eugene, OR

Mary Reeve
Educator
Gallup McKinley County Schools
Gallup, NM

Autism Ambassadors Mission Statement

Autism is a pervasive condition that affects millions of children in the United States and abroad. This year, anywhere from 1 out of every 150 to 1 out of every 64 children will be diagnosed with one of the autism spectrum disorders (ASDs). These children will go through life stigmatized and rejected unless our system drastically changes. Autism Ambassadors aims to help children on the autism spectrum feel socially connected to, and integrated in, their academic environments by teaching these children to build sustainable, real friendships with typical children.

Autism Ambassadors Vision Statement

To lower the barriers that prevent children with autism from participating in the school system as fully functioning members.

About the Author

 **Zak Kukoff** is an 18-year-old social entrepreneur based in Westlake Village, California, and, at the time of this printing, a senior at Westlake High School. Zak is the founder of Autism Ambassadors, a nonprofit that builds friendships between students with special needs and typical students in more than 25 schools throughout the United States and abroad. In his spare time, he volunteers at the Westminster Free Clinic, which provides free medical services for those without healthcare. He also writes for the *Huffington Post* Education Section and helps organize both TEDxConejo and TEDxYouth@ Conejo. He previously founded the education-technology startup TruantToday. His work has been featured in the *New York Times*, TechCrunch, Bloomberg View, The Next Web, and other well-known publications, and has been honored by the Clinton Global Initiative and NBC Education Nation. Contact him on twitter: @zck.

PART I

The Program

*There are those who look at things the way they are, and ask "why" ...
I dream of things that never were, and ask "why not?"*

—Robert F. Kennedy

1

Autism and Society Today

Autism is an epidemic. You've probably heard that discussed on the news, in television shows, or online somewhere. But what does that mean, exactly? Well, before we answer that question, before we really get into why this is such a hot-button topic in everything from academic think tanks to the *Today* show, let's take a look at a few statistics that should give you an indication of just exactly how extensive the problem is:

- Every 20 minutes, sports radio stations simulcast an update.
- Every 20 minutes, an average of 20 kites are made.
- Every 20 minutes, a child is diagnosed with autism (according to the Parker Autism Foundation and numerous other sources).

Every 20 minutes, a child is diagnosed with autism. I don't know about you, but when I heard that statistic, especially when put in context with those other statistics, I was amazed. Every 20 minutes. That's a pretty short span of time. It means that, depending on how fast a reader you are, from the time you started reading this introduction to right now, at least one child with autism entered this world.

As I mentioned in my introduction, autism is a pervasive developmental disorder that affects millions of children in the United States and abroad. To watch kids, or adults, with autism is to watch people engaging in behaviors that can seem strange to most people: hand-flapping, toe-walking, an obsession with certain colors or objects to the exclusion of everything else, and a seeming obliviousness to the world around them. To define autism in neurological terms, however, let's first learn a little bit about how the brain works. In the brains of typical students, both hemispheres work together. They pass information back and forth, like two partners working on a project, or like two students crunching a deadline together. Each side has its responsibilities, and those responsibilities are met through extensive, lightning-fast teamwork. In the brains of students with autism, however, the two hemispheres work simultaneously, side by side, but not together. This means that the information that needs to be passed back and forth isn't shared the way it should be. To put that another way, imagine trying to listen to two songs at the same time, instead of one song right after the other. That's what most information sounds like—and the way the world looks—to students with autism, every single day of their lives.

As I also said earlier, the number of students diagnosed with autism at present is exponentially higher than it was in generations past. Some people feel that the root cause is something in the environment or something that was transmitted through a batch of bad vaccines. Others claim that the increase is due in some part to more fine-tuned diagnostic tools used by psychologists and doctors; we are simply more aware of the symptoms and therefore are catching more cases than we used to, giving people a diagnosis of autism when, a generation ago, they simply would have been labeled as "strange" or not labeled at all. As far as I'm concerned, I don't really care why the numbers are as high as they are; all I know is that they are and that I care to do whatever I can to make the existing situation better. Because along with autism's emotional toll, which is immeasurable, there are other statistics that are nothing short of overwhelming when you think about them:

- According to a 2012 study funded by Autism Speaks (2012a) and conducted by researchers at the University of Pennsylvania and the London School of Economics, autism, with its considerable toll on school and social resources, costs over $137 billion, a cost that is expected to increase dramatically in the years to come.
- According to the Centers for Disease Control (Autism Speaks, 2012b), more children will be diagnosed with autism this year than with AIDS, diabetes, and cancer combined, and while psychologists and educators have made great strides in their respective fields, there is no medical cure for autism.

So why is this important? After all, everyone can read the paragraph above and conclude that it is sad, but sad conclusions alone, sadly enough, do not necessarily lead to action. Well, that's where we come in. Autism Ambassadors' philosophy is that, without a medical cure, programs like ours are the most effective way to raise the quality of life for students with special needs. We feel that, given how pervasive autism is in the worldwide community, autism is everyone's responsibility, not only the responsibility of health care and educational professionals and parents with afflicted children. Virtually everyone knows someone with autism, which means that it is not some obscure medical affliction that can be ignored by the majority. At Autism Ambassadors, the key question that we ask ourselves is, if we don't help, who will?

And where does all of this start? With the teacher, the concerned parent, the administrator, and, most of all, you—the student.

2

Typical Students and Students With Autism

Before designing and implementing a nationwide—and, ultimately, international—program that paired up typical students with students with autism, I thought it was important to get a sense for how students with autism were seen by their peers. I spent a great deal of time talking with psychologists and educators, but I spent an even greater amount of time talking with typical students who came into contact with students with autism, day after day. I wanted to hear what people felt in the hallways, in their cafeterias, on the playgrounds, and in their classrooms. I asked question after question, took personal surveys, and sent out hundreds of e-mails to students at schools all over the world. What I found didn't surprise me so much as it gave me food for thought. The schools might have been different, but the responses were mostly the same; everywhere I went, students reported as follows:

They feel sorry for their classmates with autism: Most students' hearts are in the right place. They truly feel sorry for students with autism who are obviously struggling with what looks to us like the most mundane tasks and easy social obligations. Most typical students, with the exception of the truly indifferent—and I don't think that's a very large number at all—can sympathize with their fellow students. But as sympathetic as they are, as sorry as they feel for these students, they cannot empathize with them. As I mentioned in the preface, empathy is different from sympathy; sympathy means simply feeling sorry for people from a distance, but empathy means understanding them from within—knowing how and why they feel, a certain way. Because most typical students' feelings end at sympathy, they expressed to me that they were not motivated to do anything to help students with autism. Autism Ambassadors teaches students how to feel empathy for students with autism and therefore how to make a meaningful and lasting impact in their lives.

They are afraid of what other people might think: We all know that peer pressure can be a major factor in how students behave toward other students. Students who find themselves in the popular clique might shun other students with whom they once played board and yard games, back before peer pressure made them self-conscious about the company they kept. This is especially true when it comes to students with autism; even though what they have is not contagious, and middle and high school students are far beyond the domain of "cooties," students with autism are frequently shunned because most typical students fear that they themselves might be called "special" or even worse by the other typical students. What is important to understand is that this behavior springs from insecurity that is sadly all too typical of the school-aged psyche. A secure student who carries him or herself with confidence can befriend whomever he or she wants with pride. (Notably, Troy Polamalu, the Hall of Fame–bound Pittsburgh Steelers safety, used to spend his lunch hours in high school helping kids with special needs—and rest assured, no one said a word to him about it.) (Sandler, 2012). Not only does Autism Ambassadors address these feelings in potential Ambassadors, but its curriculum aims to change how students with autism are perceived so as to negate the corrosive effects of negative peer pressure. (I will talk more about the potential positive effects of peer pressure in the next chapter.)

They do not know how to interact with their classmates with autism: Believe it or not, many typical students are actually scared of students with autism. We are conditioned to fear that which strikes us as different or, as we perceive the behavior in these cases, alien. And these students' behaviors are so alien to most typical students that they give in to their gut-level reaction, which is to turn and walk away from anything that strikes them as weird or "off." Students with autism are seemingly indifferent to their surroundings, or to matters of social etiquette and/or hygiene, and their anxiety levels are so high that they don't typically initiate social behavior. So without an ambassadorial presence, typical students and students with autism are like two ships passing in the night. Autism Ambassadors bridges these gaps so that these two ships stop, meet, and embark on the rest of their journey together.

The kids who do want to help don't know how: The more time I spent developing the Autism Ambassadors curriculum, the more it became clear that interacting with students with autism was so overwhelming that most typical students didn't even know how, or where, to begin. Autism Ambassadors' lesson plans give students the means to break down social behaviors into small, easily understood parts of social behavior that virtually anyone with the right motivation can implement. And once their peers watch Ambassadors' behavior around students with autism, it becomes contagious and ultimately second nature to even non-Ambassadors.

3

The Importance of Peer Leadership

What the Research Says

It is more or less a given that kids follow the examples set by other kids, both good and bad, which, conventional wisdom dictates, mostly comprises the latter. After all, we are always hearing that familiar phrase, "peer pressure," whenever we are being told by counselors not to do drugs, or to drink and drive, or to be sexually promiscuous. But as easy as it is to talk about the negative aspects of peer pressure, I believe that the opposite is also true—that it is just as easy to find teenagers setting positive examples for their peers to follow, and subsequently recruiting those peers to do good. On this subject, I am happy to say that I speak from experience; last year, I was the recipient of Ventura County's "Awesome in Autism" award for my work with this organization, and at the awards banquet I had the good fortune to talk to over a dozen kids just like me.

The million dollar question, however, did not concern typical students; it concerned students with autism. As I have pointed out, I am optimistic that many typical students can and do follow strong leaders who are all about doing right by their peers. Strangely enough, the question concerned the students with autism. I wanted to find out if these students, who seem basically indifferent to, or ignorant of, their surroundings—and by extension their peers—could be affected by peer pressure. At first blush, my eyes told me one thing, although my gut told me another thing entirely. I had watched my family member Sara for years, and I knew that just because she didn't seem to be paying attention didn't mean that she wasn't quietly filing away information about all the behavior she was witnessing. My feeling was that many of these kids were like Sara—they wanted to fit in; they just didn't know how. And the more I looked around, the more I researched, the more I was convinced that I was right.

So what did that mean? I started looking around at what schools were doing, and the more I looked the more I kept reading about peer leadership groups. Peer leadership—an extremely effective system of programs that enable teenagers to teach themselves and each other methods to better their academic, social, and behavioral circumstances—is an idea whose versatility and scope is just now being fully realized. The success of peer leadership groups all over the country has provided sociologists with some of the most promising data on how students can use accessible social and behavioral programs to help themselves and their fellow teenagers. Schools have peer leadership groups to address everything from drug abuse to bullying, but prior to the creation of Autism Ambassadors, nowhere was there a peer leadership group whose mission statement was to tackle perhaps the most pervasive developmental issue of our generation: autism.

Consider this quote from a professional journal about autism and developmental disorders:

> Many students with autism are being served in inclusive settings. Early intervention programs, traditionally home-based, are beginning to create center-based options which incorporate typically developing peers. One of the arguments for the use of inclusive programs is that students with autism will benefit from their exposure to and interactions with typical peers. (Laushey & Heflin, 2000, p. 183)

Clearly other individuals, independent of each other, recognize the power of typical peer interaction and are taking steps in the right direction to incorporate typical students into programs that, in the past, have been inclusive only of students with autism. However, simple exposure is not enough; Laushey and Heflin go on to add that "unfortunately, research suggests that in inclusive settings, typical peers and peers with autism do not always interact without prompting from an adult" (2000, pp. 183–193). As we have seen, however, that adult might be preoccupied, or ill equipped, or overwhelmed, or not present.

So what is the answer? Well, after analyzing one approach in which typical students and students with autism were mixed together and then were left simply to fend for themselves, the study went on to describe two other approaches in which the typical students were given set prompts and objectives for the students with autism.

> The second approach consists of operant training in which the peers are taught to prompt a response from the student with autism and then to reinforce the desired behavior (Odom & Strain, 1984; Roeyers, 1996). The third approach is a peer-initiated procedure in which the peer tutors are instructed and trained to make social initiations to the target students (Odom, Hoyson, Jamieson, & Strain, 1985). (Laushey & Heflin, 2000, p. 184)

The study found that while any social interaction was beneficial for the students with autism, it also went on to say that

> research indicates that the second and third approaches are typically more effective in teaching specific skills to the student with autism (Roeyers, 1996) . . . students with autism have deficits in social skills. Peer tutoring has been shown to produce positive effects in teaching more appropriate social skills to students with autism. (Laushey & Heflin, 2000, p. 184.)

This is where the guiding principles of Autism Ambassadors come in. Researchers agreed that there needed to be more actual interaction between typical students and students with autism, but if the students with autism are to reap the maximum benefit from this interaction, there needs to be some formal training program available to the typical students.

> It is predicted that training peers (Odom et al., 1985) rather than simply placing students with autism in close proximity to peers will facilitate increased demonstration of social skills in the students with autism (Odom & Strain, 1984; Roeyers, 1996). (Laushey & Heflin, 2000, p. 184)

And clearly Laushey and Heflin agreed that, for the program to succeed on any wide-scale basis, it would need to involve a commensurate percentage of the typical population:

> It is also predicted that training an entire class of peers, including those with autism, will assist in the generalization of social skills (Strain et al., 1984) and incorporate a contextual approach in naturalistic settings. (Laushey & Heflin, 2000, pp. 184-185)

This was some of the most comprehensive research I could get my hands on, performed by leaders in the field of autism research, and it was confirming what my gut was telling me: The best way to take on this epidemic at the school level wasn't to make the teachers do more (they are already overburdened as it is) or hire more special needs aides (with budgets being slashed, there's simply no money in any school district for even modest hires), but rather to use our most cost-effective, powerful resources: our fellow students.

4

Who and What Is Autism Ambassadors?

By now you should have a pretty good sense of who I am and what it is that led to the creation of Autism Ambassadors. So now let me define for you exactly who and what Autism Ambassadors is, what it is we do, and why we are different from any other peer leadership group.

Autism Ambassadors is a peer leadership group made up of highly committed young students dedicated to changing the way autism is viewed in the classroom and in society as a whole. The Autism Ambassadors curriculum, which I developed with a licensed clinical psychologist who has been kind enough to serve as a professional volunteer, teaches students everything from basic everyday hygiene to advanced social skills. It is free to join, costs nothing for schools to implement, and, as of this printing, is being used in dozens of elementary, middle, and high schools all over this country as well as throughout the world. It is a dynamic new educational and social initiative that aims to make students with autism feel comfortable in school, which, by extension, will enable them to lead a more mainstream-friendly lifestyle.

Autism Ambassadors is operated based on a buddy system that helps students with autism assimilate more easily into mainstream classrooms. Typical students gain a greater appreciation of students with autism, and together they develop respectful relationships that help change the way autism is viewed in the classroom as well as in society as a whole. In addition, when typical-student buddies help students with autism, teachers (whose classes grow increasingly larger after fourth grade) can spread their time among many students who may need assistance, instead of focusing simply on one or two students with autism. If a teacher has one or more students with autism in class, there is a high likelihood that one or more of those students will require continuous, in-class assistance. This is due to the increasing demands placed on teachers to include students with autism in their classes, the growing complexity of the average school curriculum, and the students with autism themselves, whose underlying social and emotional dynamics become more evident to their teachers, their peers, and themselves as they grow up.

This presents the following problems:

1. Students with autism tend to get lost or become disoriented in a classroom environment.

2. Teachers' aides and shadows, who often work with students with autism out of necessity in many cases, can also further stigmatize these students.

3. Aides and shadows cost school districts enormous sums of money, and, due to a variety of factors from insufficient training to insufficient motivation, don't always yield the results that we would ideally like to see.

The social challenges of students with autism can make a typical day an even greater challenge for both teachers and students. Autism Ambassadors provides a curriculum that trains typical students to interact daily with students with autism, either in their Autism Ambassadors class or in other classes in their schools. The Ambassador sits with the student with autism for at least one hour per day to help that student focus, as well as ensure that the student is not being teased, bullied, or distracted by any other outside factors. This approach helps all parties involved for the following reasons:

1. The student with autism learns the kind of social and academic skills that will help him function better in mainstream classrooms.

2. The Ambassador learns to appreciate firsthand the challenges that her partner faces while learning the true definition of empathy.

3. Teachers are required to spend less time keeping students with autism on task and can devote their resources to other matters.

Not only that, the overinvolvement of aides and shadows can be downright detrimental. To quote from the conclusion of the Laushey and Heflin study discussed in Chapter 3,

> The outcomes of the study demonstrate that advocates for students with autism need to carefully consider how to support the potential benefits from placement in inclusive settings. The use of a "shadow" or adult assistant in inclusive settings has been criticized for inhibiting social interactions and resulting in prompt dependency in children with autism. (Giangreco, Edelman, Luiselli, & MacFarland, 1997). (Laushey & Heflin, 2000, p. 192)

Again, the evidence points strongly in the same direction that Autism Ambassadors is facing: "Social interactions, occurring between children with autism and their peers, may be best supported when all are trained in pro-social exchanges and provided the necessary structure to promote success" (Laushey & Heflin, 2000, p. 192).

Autism Ambassadors is the first peer leadership group that takes typical peers and matches them up with their fellow students with autism to create real, sustainable friendships. Not only is Autism Ambassadors unique in this sense, it is also different in another regard: It is not a school-sanctioned organization, but rather a dynamic new youth movement started and propagated at the grass roots level. While there is always faculty oversight, students themselves are the leaders responsible for developing and implementing the curriculum and providing feedback to the organization. We want to hear from you; we are always making changes to our programs and are always interested in hearing what is and is not working on your end. (Note our questionnaires and related appendices at the end of this book.)

Our goals are academically and behaviorally complex (see our curriculum for details), but also philosophically simple. We aim to build real and sustainable friendships so that we can not only teach social, emotional, and academic skills to students with autism, but also increase empathy and understanding inside and outside the classroom. In doing so, Autism Ambassadors strives to lower the social and emotional barriers that prevent students with autism from interacting fully with society as a whole. As odd as it sounds, our ultimate goal is to help students with autism become so comfortable in society—and for society to become so comfortable with students with autism—that the need for Autism Ambassadors is eliminated entirely. Such a development is contrary to the desires of members of most extracurricular clubs and organizations, but it is one that all my fellow Ambassadors and I would be thrilled to see!

Many schools and interdenominational places of worship require students to compile community service hours, and these students may be interested in participating in Autism Ambassadors. We recruit students from student government classes, students in gifted student groups, and other exceptional students. They apply on an individual basis, and we teach them specific skills as outlined in our curriculum.

All Ambassadors are interviewed and screened before they meet the students with autism, and they receive weeks of extensive training with our unique curriculum. During the training period, Ambassadors learn about autism's outward manifestations and how it affects the brain, as well as basic techniques of applied behavior analysis for working with students with autism.

The students with autism are introduced to their Ambassadors and get to know them gradually through a series of initial meetings in which they learn the curriculum and are supervised by a staff member. When the Ambassadors are ready to interact with their assigned students, they "graduate" to their daily Ambassador assignment and start implementing our curriculum.

Our process is simple, yet complex at the same time; in applying our generation's most valuable resources (ourselves) toward one of our generation's neediest resources (students with autism), we create a situation that could best be described as a win/win/win. The students with autism feel happier and become more productive, the Ambassadors learn valuable empathy tools that will benefit them in every social and emotional (and ultimately professional) aspect of their lives, and the schools save money and time on resources that can be allocated to make up shortfalls in other areas like libraries, arts programs, and additional teacher hires.

5

What Is an Ambassador?

For those of you who would like to know where the name Autism Ambassadors came from, it was inspired by my love of government and politics, which have been passions of mine since I was younger. (Robert Kennedy's quote on my first section heading sums up my feelings on the subject pretty nicely.) As I read about international politics—yes, I admit it; I was an elementary school policy wonk—I kept coming across the term *ambassador*. In the political sense, an ambassador is someone who shuttles back and forth from country to country, trying to keep all parties involved on good terms based on proper communication. I thought that this was an excellent definition of what it was I wanted to do with Autism Ambassadors, right down to the international shuttle diplomacy part. (This is literally true; as of this printing, Autism Ambassadors is in Australia and Canada and is making inroads into other countries.) I viewed relations between typical students and students with autism the way I would view relations between two countries who just didn't understand each other and needed help from an outside party to communicate better.

So what does this mean for you, the student? Well, as I said in the introduction, if you're even reading this book in the first place, you are probably the kind of person who embodies exactly what it is we are looking for in an Ambassador. So let me list the qualities we typically seek out in people that make them excellent candidates for Autism Ambassadors. You are

Someone who is truly inspired to help others: I don't know about you, but I have read more than my fair share of articles that claim that our generation is the most self-involved, narcissistic, me-first generation yet.

I couldn't disagree with this more; I have been to dozens of schools all over the country and have held Skype conferences and training sessions with others all over the world, and I have had the good fortune to have encountered hundreds of students who epitomize what I'm talking about here. You are someone who really cares about his fellow students and is willing to sacrifice the occasional lunch hour or three to prove it.

Someone who has a history of commitment in other areas: How many people do you know who think that it would be nice to help out others? An Autism Ambassador is the kind of person who, rather than thinking about doing something for the good of her community, actually gets out and does it. He or she—and by that I mean you—is active in afterschool mentorship programs, religious organizations, entrepreneurial and sports-related organizations, science fair projects, children's birthday parties, camp counseling, and a whole host of other activities that require hard work, tremendous people skills, and significant follow-through abilities. You are the kind of person who sees a problem and, rather than simply opening your mouth about it, wraps your mind around it until you have hatched a solution.

Someone who is comfortable interacting with peers with autism: Most of your peers see someone with autism and duck their heads or move away. Even if they don't mean to be hurtful or exclusionary, they don't feel comfortable approaching, or interacting with, a student with autism. You are the kind of person who sees past the tics and obsessive behavior and realizes that underneath the seemingly uninterested exterior is a kid, just like you, struggling to fit in, overwhelmed by a world that almost always doesn't make sense. You may not always know exactly what's going on inside his mind, but you will do your best to try to understand your partner with autism. Ambassadors can't bridge every communication gap or challenge they face, but they almost always leave behind a situation that is better thanks to their involvement.

Someone who is willing to learn and perform the roles of both leader and follower: You might have heard the phrase, "Too many chiefs, not enough Indians" (or, to put it more diplomatically, "not enough Native Americans"). Well, that might be the case in most groups, but it is not in Autism Ambassadors. We go more by the credo of "There are no small parts, only small actors," and there are no small actors in Autism Ambassadors. Every Ambassador is expected to be both leader and follower, because our lesson plans require that kind of versatility. You might find yourself playing lead Ambassador during our **Raise Your Hand** lesson plan. Or playing the student with autism during **Riding the Bus.** Or functioning more as an extra during one of our many cafeteria-based lesson plans. The point is that no matter what is asked of you, you're not only capable of but willing to play your part.

Someone who wants to learn and improve herself: It's a given that the gift of giving is the greatest gift of all. It's a given that Ambassadors give to their peers and, in doing so, improve themselves. But Autism Ambassadors is much, much more than simply a charitable organization.

The fact that our program takes place in schools underscores the fact that Autism Ambassadors is an opportunity to learn, not only about autism and its manifold mysteries, but about everything from how the brain works neurologically to how people interact behaviorally.

Someone who wants to partner with a student who possesses similar interests: While students with autism might not present the same way their typical peers do, their behaviors do not hide the fact that underneath their surface differences they possess many of the same traits as their typical peers. Which means they love basketball. They love popular music. They love to dance, act, sing, follow politics, build things, and go to movies. Autism Ambassadors starts its mentoring process from a place of compatibility by pairing Ambassadors with like-minded peers, thus getting them off on a solid footing and helping them build real, long-term sustainable friendships.

And most of all? Someone who is great at having a good time: Okay, we're not talking life of the party here. What I mean is that there are people who always seem to be having fun, no matter where they go (just as there are people who always seem miserable, no matter how fun an environment they are in). If you are one of those people who looks at the glass as being half full, who knows how to make lemonade out of lemons (but preferably not mountains out of molehills), then Autism Ambassadors wants you. You are the type of person who joins a group because you truly think it will be fun, or eye-opening, or educational, or all three. And not just because you think it will look good on your college resume. It will, but trust us; colleges are pretty good at weeding out the people who join groups just for the prestige. You are the type of person whose enthusiasm is infectious, not only to the student with autism but to the typical student as well. In short, you are the epitome of the qualities we listed above.

6

Autism Ambassadors at Your School

The Nuts and Bolts of Implementation

So now that you've digested our message, let's talk a little bit about who and what you're going to be looking for, and the concrete steps you will need to take to create an Autism Ambassadors club at your school.

STUDENT INVOLVEMENT

Step One: Identify a Student Leader

We all know the kind of person I am talking about here. You have seen him in the movies, or on TV; heck, I have seen him in every single training session I have done, and I have done dozens to date. I am talking about the student who always comes to class prepared, sits either in or near the front row, and always seems to be raising her hand, either because she knows the answer to a question or wishes to ask one of her own. Rather than rolling your eyes at this person (remember: positive, not negative peer pressure), let's see this person for who he is: yes, an influencer, the first person picked out by teachers to help outside of class, but in a broader sense he is the kind of person who wants to stand out in the world. Which is the first quality your student leader needs. A student leader should

• Have a history of the kind of commitment that will translate into finding other students—both typical and those with autism—interested in becoming Ambassadors. A student leader is the kind of person you see holding clipboards in school hallways, or outside supermarkets, trying to get people to sign up for everything from pep rallies to voting.

• Embody a "buck stops here" mentality; rather than complain or chastise a student who did not fulfill an obligation, the student leader simply buckles down and takes care of the obligation herself. Most important, a student leader understands that politics is an admirable career path but a detriment to any organization if it is a prevailing dynamic among its members.

• Understand that leadership doesn't always mean making one's voice the loudest but rather making sure that everyone is heard and that the final decision is the right one. A student leader should be the kind of person who understands that power and toughness are often found in the person who says the least but knows how to use his words as economically and wisely as possible.

• Feel a sense of obligation to the cause not only philosophically, but morally. Autism Ambassadors came about because I had a family member with autism; while it helps to know the problem on which you are working firsthand, it is not a prerequisite. What is a prerequisite for a student leader is feeling something inside when she does the right thing. Which doesn't mean crying every time the ASPCA commercial with Sarah McLachlan comes on, but ideally it should mean that a part of your heart must be invested in this if you are going to be willing to go the extra mile when necessary, with a smile on your face to boot.

And in the absence of any of the above? A student leader should possess an excellent sense of how, and to whom, to delegate authority. Sometimes simply picking the best people is nine-tenths of the battle.

Step Two: Find a Student Committee

Your chosen student leader should appoint the student committee. The student committee's job is to

• Run the day-to-day program itself. Members of the committee should be the kind of committed, hard-working students who stay after school for study groups and make adults wring their hands about how overprogrammed today's youth is. (Okay, I'm kidding about that last part—mostly.)

• Spearhead recruiting efforts. While your chosen student leader should oversee recruiting, the truth is that it is every Ambassador's responsibility to recruit committed students for the cause. Remember, depending on your school's size and demographic makeup, there are hundreds of underserved peers out there, and hundreds more people who are able to—and want to—help but don't know where to start. Like many things, finding the right people is a numbers game; it's no different from selling products door-to-door.

• Plan and follow through on all outside efforts, including fundraising and communication. This will include everything from checking in regularly with the faculty advisor to coordinating the club's efforts with the administration to ensure that there are no problems should the club wish to hold an event on school grounds. The student committee should also be the liaison to any parent groups who might be interested in helping the club with anything from community outreach to fundraising efforts.

Step Three: Set Up an Autism Ambassadors Training!

As much as it might feel like you are processing a lot of information right now, this process isn't nearly as overwhelming as it sounds. We will happily provide an experienced Ambassador, free of charge (Autism Ambassadors is a free service; there are no dues or other costs of any kind) to help train your new students. Once they are trained, we will continue to provide guidance on how to run your club based on the peer leadership model outlined in this book.

Because we like to keep our curriculum and program as up to date as possible, once every six months we will use our proprietary evaluation tool (a copy of which can be found at the end of this book) to make sure that your Ambassadors are adhering to our curriculum and vice versa; we want our curriculum to work optimally for your club as well and welcome any feedback or suggestions you might have to improve it.

FACULTY AND ADMINISTRATION INVOLVEMENT

Every school has its own set of rules and protocol by which students and the community must abide. Autism Ambassadors feels strongly about its role as a stress-reliever, not stress-inducer, and to that end we insist that every club act in strict accordance with any and all guidelines set forth by your school's administration. While nothing inherent to Autism Ambassadors has ever created, nor should it ever create, conflict at any school of which we are a part, here are a few steps that will ensure that your club remains a member in good standing of your school community.

Step One: Get a Faculty Advisor

Most clubs require one, but just in case your school is that one exception that doesn't, we strongly urge you to have faculty oversight. As you will notice when you read our lesson plans, at times there is a behavioral factor in the training that is best addressed when a faculty member is, if not present, at least aware of the training. Autism Ambassadors is very much an educational club, which is different from being a movie lovers club; as such, it is a club for which faculty involvement has the potential to be emphasized more than it might be in other clubs. Try to recruit a faculty member who strikes you as being a slightly older version of what you look for in an Ambassador: positive and community conscious. Based on my own experience, you can usually tell if a faculty person is community conscious because he will typically be involved in student activities in his spare time. Make sure he is kept in the loop on all of the group's progress; weekly meetings are ideal, but whoever is in charge of communications should be sending out regular e-mails as well. Your faculty advisor will not only ensure that you are following all the rules but can also be a valuable resource and liaison between you and the parents (whose involvement we will soon discuss).

Step Two: Keep the Principal, or Vice Principal, Updated

Many students feel that the principal is too busy for them, or they have such a negative association with what it means to be in her office that they would rather keep what they're doing under the radar. If those are your feelings, I strongly urge you to buck them. Your principal, or if your school is too large for any real input from her, your vice principal, can be not only your biggest fan but can also be your greatest advocate in the community. (Remember, you are essentially offering her unpaid labor—by individuals who are happy to be unpaid—that will free up her other resources.) My principal, Ron Lipari, has been an advocate of Autism Ambassadors from day one and has provided me with advice and help on everything from the bureaucracy of education to handling media requests. So learn to view the administration as your friend, and make sure you keep an apple nice and shiny for those trips to the principal's office!

Step Three: Get the Parents Involved

What your student committee is to your club, your parents—and the parents not only of other Ambassadors but of students with autism—can be for your community. Think about all those Girl Scout and soccer moms and dads and how passionate they are: up early in the morning in foul weather, either to help sell boxes of cookies or help register kids for leagues. Now think about how that same work force can help your cause. While Autism Ambassadors is free, like every organization, it benefits from money and awareness. The more money that is brought in, the more the club has the freedom to actually hire extra faculty for additional hands-on help, rather than simply relying on volunteers. The more awareness that is spread through flyers, phone calls, and e-mails, the more your club can direct its resources—you—toward the people who need it most. Finding parents who wish to get involved can be a bit of a challenge; just like us, many of them are overprogrammed these days and have more commitments than they can handle. That said, parents of students with autism are typically so grateful for Autism Ambassadors that they find the time to get involved. Make them your first calls when you start signing up students with autism, and make sure your communications head maintains an updated phone number and e-mail address list at all times.

7

Curriculum Overview

Okay, so now you've got a pretty good sense of who and what we are and who and what we're looking for when it comes to Ambassadors. So now it's time to talk a little bit about our curriculum, which is the life-blood of Autism Ambassadors. This curriculum was developed over years of working with licensed clinical psychologists, all of whom generously donated their time and efforts to ensure that my lesson plans were as comprehensive as possible. Before I delve into the nuts and bolts of how it works, however, I'd like to fill you in on some of the philosophical tenets behind those nuts and bolts.

I designed the Autism Ambassadors curriculum based on my personal experience with a close relative diagnosed with autism. We have an advisory board of psychologists to help oversee the implementation of the curriculum, which is composed of a combination of social and emotional lessons that pertain to the natural scheduling of the academic day.

The Autism Ambassadors curriculum was designed to ensure that everyone has the opportunity to be friends with a student with autism. Typical students normally stay away from students with autism because they don't know how to react when a student with autism does something unusual or different. We want to make sure there are no excuses, so we use our curriculum to train Ambassadors to know what to do in these situations. Most important, as Ambassadors, we want to join the world of our friends with autism, rather than simply having them join ours.

The Autism Ambassadors curriculum utilizes the idea of role-playing, one of the most natural forms of interaction for all ages. When we are little, we play house, dress-up, and firemen, and when we get older, we act in school plays and school projects. This technique of interchangeable role-playing, in addition to teaching the Ambassador how to interact with a student with autism, helps create an empathy link between the Ambassador and the student with autism.

The Autism Ambassadors curriculum is divided into individual lesson plans, or modules, that are designed to be integrated into the different segments of the school day. They replicate the natural social interaction that students will ultimately have with the student with autism.

The Autism Ambassadors curriculum works best when it is kept up to date; to achieve this end, we ask all Ambassadors and students with autism to fill out our proprietary evaluation tool (included at the end of this book). The evaluation tool was created by a student with autism and was edited and shaped by our executive student advisory board. We feel strongly that this is the best way to ensure that our curriculum continues to make concrete changes in the lives of students with autism.

Additionally, the students with autism have their progress monitored through a detailed questionnaire that is distributed two times: once before the Ambassador's training begins, and once at the midpoint of the Ambassador's training. The questionnaires are given to the people who come in contact most with the student with autism: teachers, family members, other caretakers, and the Ambassador who is paired up with the student with autism.

Additional details about the curriculum can be found in the modules themselves, as well as in the FAQ's section at the end of this book.

PART II
The Curriculum

There is only one thing for it then—to learn. Learn why the world wags and what wags it. That is the only thing which the mind can never exhaust, never alienate, never be tortured by, never fear or distrust, and never dream of regretting. Learning is the only thing for you. Look what a lot of things there are to learn.

—T. H. White, *The Once and Future King*

Modules for Younger/Lower Functioning Students

While most of the students who benefit from the Autism Ambassadors curriculum are middle or high school aged, there are still a great number who are significantly younger—in kindergarten through fifth grade, and in some cases, preschool aged. In addition, because autism is a developmental disorder, age is not always the key factor in determining a student's level of functionality. Sadly, a great number of high school and even college aged students need to use the modules outlined in this handbook on a daily basis, as they have not generalized many of the lower level skills that their peers, even many of those with autism, take for granted. Many other students with autism, while having a basic command of these modules, will still require the occasional tune-up at various points in their day-to-day activities. Even for Ambassadors who won't ever wind up using them, these modules are good to know, because they form the foundation of many other modules.

The five modules that make up this section for younger or lower functioning students are as follows:

1. Pay Attention/Calm Hands

2. Being Alone

3. Logical Sequencing

4. Passing the Baton

5. Washing Hands at School

Pay Attention/Calm Hands is one of the staples of any ABA (applied behavior analysis) program and is one of the underlying modules to which

Ambassadors should refer whenever they are having a difficult time keeping students with autism engaged. Getting students with autism to pay attention (or "attend" as it is clinically known) can be extremely difficult, yet it is the most important task they all must generalize if they are to have success with any further modules. And many students with autism exhibit self-stimulatory behavior ("stims"), of which flapping hands is one of the most common; this, too, must be addressed if the students are to have any success implementing an ABA-based program.

Being Alone addresses the intense feelings of isolation a student with autism sometimes feels when he does not have a buddy by his side. Students with autism need to be able to separate from both parents when they begin attending school, and, while working with an Ambassador can be a wonderful "baby step" on the way to realizing this goal, the Ambassador cannot be the student's constant companion at all times during the school day. This module helps students with autism to feel secure when they need to be alone or unaccompanied during school hours.

Logical Sequencing addresses the building blocks of basic story-telling. Again, this is a staple of any ABA-based curriculum, as it speaks to the essential need of a story (or, for that matter, any series of events) to be told in linear, logical progression. There are a great number of fully functioning adults who struggle with this skill; imagine how difficult it must be for a student with autism, whose cranial hemispheres do not interact with each other the way they do in typical brains.

Passing the Baton extends the principles introduced in Pay Attention/ Calm Hands. The underlying objective—namely to tell a story in a linear fashion—is upheld, but in this exercise we introduce a back-and-forth dynamic (ergo the "baton" in the module's title) between the student and the Ambassador. This promotes not only creative thinking but also the kind of collaboration that will be necessary for students when they reach high school and need to engage with large- or medium-sized groups of their peers, who will want to discuss everything from last night's *American Idol* to the events that transpired at a recent weekend party.

Washing Hands at School is a seemingly simple module that has far-reaching ramifications for students with tactile issues, especially those that concern water. Because schools are veritable petri dishes for spreading germs, hygiene is extremely important; all students should be in the habit of washing their hands numerous times daily, especially given the number of door handles, locker panels, cafeteria trays, other students' hands, et cetera with which they come into contact. Beyond that, sensitivity to the sensation of water on one's skin can be an impediment socially; many students enjoy pool or beach parties in their spare time, and an inability to engage in water-based activities only isolates the student with autism even more than he already is.

Pay Attention/ Calm Hands

*An Autism Ambassadors
Original Module*

Intro

The goal of this module is to instruct Ambassadors how to teach proper social etiquette for students (especially younger students) with autism to use when they need to work with others, focus, and keep their often-active hands still.

Many students with autism have increased anxiety levels caused by external stimuli; everything from noises (even certain forms of otherwise pleasurable music) to lights or the feeling of someone's fingers on their skin can create distress for these students. This foundation-level module, which Ambassadors can and should refer to whenever the students with whom they are working lose focus or allow their self-stimulatory behavior to get the better of them, will teach students how to be less vulnerable to outside distractions.

The module can take place in a school lunch area or library; anywhere the Ambassador and student can work in relative peace and quiet. We will require other students to role-play everything from the student with autism to random students who will be passing by from time to time. In addition, the Ambassadors will need a small, sticky gold star and some other objects (Frisbee, paddleball toy, etc.) that can be used as potential tools of distraction.

We are now ready to begin. The Ambassador and the student with autism enter the work area and sit down.

AMBASSADOR:	(Student's name), today we are going to practice looking at each other and keeping our hands calm.
STUDENT:	[flaps hands]
AMBASSADOR:	Let's play a game: When I say "calm hands," let's count to five. We are going to keep our hands calm for five seconds; then we can flap them all we want.

Students with autism frequently exhibit signs of self-stimulatory behavior, or *stims,* such as flapping hands, whenever they are asked to perform tasks for which they feel unprepared or anxious. While ideally use of these stims will subside with age and maturity, it is by no means a given that that will be the case. The goal of this exercise is to give the student an outlet through which to use her stim and therefore keep it contained in a less socially unacceptable place.

STUDENT: Okay.

AMBASSADOR: Okay, ready, set, go—calm hands.

Verbal prompts, such as "calm hands" or "pay attention" are important and must be issued each time, as they will become the prompt to which the student will become conditioned to answer in the future.

AMBASSADOR: One, two, three, four, five. Good calm hands! Now you can flap!

STUDENT: [flaps her hands]

AMBASSADOR: Great job waiting! Okay, now let's do the same thing, only for ten seconds.

STUDENT: [flaps hands]

Counting is an effective device with which to teach self-control and focus to students with autism; it gives them a psychological tool to measure the length of any given part of the exercise and allows them to channel all of their focus into one part of the task while blocking out the other, more unpleasant parts of the task.

AMBASSADOR: You can flap your hands, but once I say "ready, set, go," we're going to keep our hands calm for ten seconds this time. Okay?

STUDENT: Okay.

AMBASSADOR: Okay, ready, set go—calm hands.

The Ambassador counts to ten; then the student flaps her hands.

AMBASSADOR: Good job waiting! Okay, now we're going to add a different part of the game: You're going to look right at me and pay attention for ten seconds. Ready, set, go—pay attention.

STUDENT: [flaps hands and looks away]

AMBASSADOR: Calm hands—one, two, three, four, five . . .

STUDENT: [whines; makes noises, but doesn't listen]

AMBASSADOR: Okay, I have an idea: Let's try that again, but this time you only have to look at me and pay attention for five seconds.

The Ambassador takes the gold star and places it on his forehead. Then he turns to the student.

AMBASSADOR: Okay, ready, set, go—pay attention...

The student looks at the star on the Ambassador's forehead as the Ambassador counts to five.

> By combining the gold star with the counting, the Ambassador has provided the student with two things to focus on. This helps the student to block out any other distractions.

AMBASSADOR: Great job! Now let's try to do that while counting to ten.

STUDENT: [flaps hands]

AMBASSADOR: Calm hands—one, two, three, four, five.

STUDENT: [relaxes her hands]

> The student has mastered calming the hands when nothing else is being asked of her. This technique should be used any time during an exercise when a student is flapping and cannot seem to control the stim.

AMBASSADOR: Good calm hands! Now let's try looking at me and counting to ten: ready, set, go—pay attention.

The Ambassador starts to count to ten, but at the five mark, another Ambassador comes by with a paddleball toy that distracts the student with autism.

AMBASSADOR: Pay attention.

The student looks back at the Ambassador but is clearly frustrated that she cannot pay attention to the student with the paddleball toy.

AMBASSADOR: I know there's a lot around us that you would like to look at, but if you can look at me for ten seconds while we count, then we can go get cookies.

> Rewards such as cookies can be used when students are having too difficult at time staying on task. (The crude term for this is *bribery,* although in this context, since it involves an extremely important objective, it can be referred to as *use of a token economy*). Ambassadors need to be aware that many students with autism have gluten/casein free diets that must be rigidly adhered to. Should that be the case with the student with whom the Ambassador is working, the Ambassador should be ready to substitute another snack.

STUDENT: Okay.

AMBASSADOR: Okay, ready, set, go—pay attention.

The student looks at the Ambassador as he counts to ten.

AMBASSADOR: Good paying attention! Good calm hands!

Outro

In order to overcome the student's fear and anxiety caused by focusing for an extended period of time, the Ambassador made good use of counting exercises, which he gradually extended until the student was able to focus for a sustained period of time. The student was tested with the types of distractions she would likely encounter in a cafeteria or lunch area but was ultimately able to focus. (Ambassadors should substitute other kinds of distractions, from Frisbee games to people actively approaching either the student or the Ambassador and trying to get their attention, as a means of bolstering the student's focusing abilities).

As with all other modules, it is imperative that Ambassadors anticipate distracting situations that might arise and use their training to refocus the student's attention back on the task at hand. If necessary, it is fine for the Ambassador to improvise, as long as the improvisation falls well within the range of acceptable behavior. Should more assistance be necessary, the Ambassador should not hesitate to engage a teacher or school supervisor.

Being Alone

An Autism Ambassadors Original Module

Intro

It is natural for all children, and perhaps all adults for that matter, to fear abandonment. Everyone wants a source of comfort that he can turn to during difficult times. For a younger student, this reassurance is especially important. However it is also important for the student to do things independently as he gets older. Over time, the student learns that even though the Ambassador may not be in the same room, she is still there as a source of comfort in times of need.

For some reason, a fear of isolation remains prevalent even into the school age years for many students with autism. **Overcoming Isolation** is a module aimed at helping the student overcome a fear of abandonment so that time away from the Ambassador is not always traumatic. The process resembles a hide-and-seek sort of game that will use baby steps toward separation as the student becomes more comfortable with the Ambassador's absence.

To begin, you will need the student's favorite object. (In the example here, it is a pencil box.) Place this object on a table, and place chairs at the table so they face away from any distracting windows or doors. If the student is already carrying the object when it is time to work, you do not need to take it away and put it on the table, but make sure the student has it when as the module gets started.

As with all of our other modules, should the student show signs of extended disengagement or display self-stimulatory behavior with his hands, the Ambassador should refer to the introductory module, **Pay Attention/Calm Hands,** in order to get the student to be fully present for the lesson.

We are now ready to begin. The Ambassador brings the student into the library and seats him in a chair. A pencil case is sitting on the table.

AMBASSADOR: (Student's name), today we are going to learn to sit by ourselves.

STUDENT: [looks away]

AMBASSADOR: Let's play with the pencil case.

The Ambassador hands the pencil case to the student.

STUDENT: [picks up the pencil case and plays with it, then bounces it along the table]

AMBASSADOR: Good job!

The Ambassador gets up from the table without saying anything and steps outside the door, still in sight of the student.

AMBASSADOR: I'm going to stand over here. You can come over to me if you like.

STUDENT: [gets up from the chair and runs to the Ambassador, still holding the pencil case]

AMBASSADOR: Good job!

The Ambassador brings the student back to the table, guiding him gently by the arm.

AMBASSADOR: [in a soothing tone] Sit down.

The Ambassador steps into the hallway, barely out of sight of the student.

STUDENT: [becomes distressed and runs into the hallway to the Ambassador]

AMBASSADOR: It's okay.

The Ambassador brings the student back to the table and sits him in the chair.

> It is likely that the student will become distressed at this point if he has difficulty with isolation. The Ambassador does not reward the student for coming to her in the hallway, because she asked the student to remain at the table. The Ambassador says a firm "no" and brings the student back to the table. Now the student learns that he must remain alone at the table until the Ambassador says it is all right to go find her.

AMBASSADOR: [more firmly this time] Sit down!

STUDENT: [sits in the chair]

AMBASSADOR: Good sitting!

The Ambassador leaves the room and goes into the hallway again. She counts to five silently and then says,

AMBASSADOR: (Student's name), where am I?

STUDENT: [quickly gets up and runs to the Ambassador]

AMBASSADOR: Good job!

The Ambassador brings the student back to the table and sits down.

The Ambassador may continue to practice these steps until the student is comfortable remaining in the library while the Ambassador is out of sight but still within earshot. Ultimately we want the student to be comfortable alone while the Ambassador is anywhere in the building. To do this, we must reassure the student that he will be able to find the Ambassador in a time of need. Once the student is comfortable with the steps we have just shown, the Ambassador may move on to the following steps.

The Ambassador leaves the room and stands within the doorway where the student can see her.

AMBASSADOR: Call me!

STUDENT: (Ambassador's name)!

AMBASSADOR: [in a friendly tone] I'm right here!

Now it is the student's turn to call out to the Ambassador.
    When the Ambassador is in plain view, she may say I'm right here. The student can look to where the voice is coming from and learn the location of the Ambassador.

STUDENT: [runs to the Ambassador]

AMBASSADOR: Good job!

The Ambassador walks the student back to the table and sits the student down. The Ambassador walks into the hallway, out of the student's view.

STUDENT: [worried] (Ambassador's name)!

AMBASSADOR: I'm in the hallway!

STUDENT: [runs to the Ambassador]

AMBASSADOR: Good job!

The Ambassador brings the student back to the table.

The student has learned to call for the Ambassador to find out where she is. Now, when the student becomes distressed because the Ambassador is out of sight, he calls out the Ambassador's name. The Ambassador answers, telling the student where she is. Even if the student does not understand where the hallway is, he can follow the Ambassador's voice.
    Continue to practice this from other parts of the hallway. If the Ambassador is somewhere else in the building that is harder to locate, the student may call out several times. The Ambassador should continue to answer with her location until the student is able to locate the Ambassador by the sound of her voice.

Outro

By taking baby steps along the way, the Ambassador can help the student become more and more comfortable with the Ambassador being out of the room. Eventually the student learns to call out to the Ambassador in order to be with her, or to simply know where the Ambassador is. However the student must also be comfortable during the times he is not with the Ambassador. Therefore the Ambassador should continue to practice this program until she is able to leave the room for several minutes before the student calls out to the Ambassador. This may take some time for certain students, but eventually they will become more comfortable alone as they learn the Ambassador is always within earshot.

As with all other modules, it is imperative that Ambassadors anticipate distracting situations that might arise and use their training to refocus the student's attention back on the task at hand. If necessary, it is fine for the Ambassador to improvise, as long as the improvisation falls well within the range of acceptable behavior. Should more assistance be necessary, the Ambassador should not hesitate to engage a teacher or school supervisor.

Logical
Sequencing

An Autism Ambassadors
Original Module

Intro

The objective of this module is to emphasize the importance of logical progressions throughout a student's daily routine by using index cards—ones that can be crudely drawn if budget and time do not permit for a set of more expensive, predesigned cards—that help teach beginnings, middles, and ends of familiar stories.

For most people, it is a given that the events of a story follow an inherent logic; telling someone that he should dry off before jumping in a pool would garner strange looks from that person. However, students with autism tend to struggle with associative reasoning, and since their brains work differently from typical brains, the events and order of a story frequently appear to have no rhyme or reason.

Our **Logical Sequencing** exercise uses picture cards (as stated previously, crude drawings or photos cut out from magazines can work as well) to represent major parts of a story that will, for the purposes of this exercise, be a story that is familiar to most. By placing these cards in the correct order, the student with autism will be able to tell a story that makes sense. Students can then ideally apply these skills to recount stories, either actual or make-believe during playtime, in their own lives. (Refer to our module **Passing the Baton** for further assistance in this area; the two modules should ideally be taught in conjunction with one another.)

For the purposes of this exercise, we will be telling the story of The Three Little Pigs and the Big Bad Wolf. Predesigned story cards can be bought in children's bookstores, on Amazon, or through other educational companies like Lakeshore, but Ambassadors can also tell basic stories using either drawings or pictures from anywhere as long as they are able to be logically sequenced.

This module takes place in a lunch room in school. To replicate a lunch room setting, we need other students, which we will select from among the students in Ambassador training. All Ambassador trainees role-play and take turns being the student who needs assistance as well as other members of the class milling about.

As with all of our other modules, should the student show signs of extended disengagement or display self-stimulatory behavior with her hands, the Ambassador should refer to our introductory module **Pay Attention/Calm Hands** in order to get the student to be fully present for the lesson.

We are now ready to begin. The Ambassador leads the student with autism over to a lunch table, and they sit down.

AMBASSADOR: (Student's name), I have a great idea: Let's play a game!

STUDENT: Okay—let's play tag. You're it!

> Although we are not headed in that direction right now, please refer to our module **Playing Tag** for further assistance with the actual game of tag, which, should the student especially enjoy the game, can be used as an incentive for succeeding in this exercise.

AMBASSADOR: I'd love to play tag with you later, but right now I'd love to play a game where we tell a story.

STUDENT: [flaps hands]

AMBASSADOR: (Student's name), I know you want to play outside, and like I said, we can play tag or whatever you want after we play our story game first. Okay?

STUDENT: Okay.

The Ambassador lays out the story cards on the table in order, so that the student can see them from beginning to end.

AMBASSADOR: This is the story of the three little pigs. Once upon a time, there were three pigs and a big bad wolf....

The Ambassador tells the entire story, using the cards, and then puts the cards back in a stack, still in order with the first card on the top.

> Even though we are telling a story that should be familiar to the student, it is still a good idea to run through the whole story first.

AMBASSADOR: Once upon a time, there were three little pigs ...

The Ambassador puts down the first picture of the three little pigs.

AMBASSADOR: There was also a big bad wolf.

The Ambassador puts down the second card with a picture of the big bad wolf.

AMBASSADOR: Can you help me tell the story? I'd really love it if you'd put the card that goes at the beginning first, then put the card that comes next right after it.

STUDENT: [whines for a moment, but then focuses and puts the cards in the correct order]

AMBASSADOR: Great job, (student's name)!

The Ambassador begins the story again, placing the first card, then the second, and this time adding the third. Then the Ambassador mixes up the three cards.

AMBASSADOR: Okay, now can you put these cards in the right order?

STUDENT: [places the cards in the correct order]

> As the Ambassador begins adding more cards, the student will likely have more difficulty putting them in order. After giving her a chance to arrange the cards independently, the Ambassador should give clues by telling parts of the story again as the student arranges the cards.

AMBASSADOR: Great job!

The Ambassador begins the story again, placing the first card, then the second, then the third, and this time adding the fourth. Then the Ambassador mixes up the four cards.

AMBASSADOR: Put these cards in order.

STUDENT: [places the cards in the correct order]

The Ambassador repeats this process until every one of the cards has been used, and then mixes up all the cards in a random arrangement on the table.

AMBASSADOR: Okay, now I really, really need help. I've lost my way. Can you point to the card that comes first?

STUDENT: [points to the wrong card]

AMBASSADOR: Wow, that's a really neat part of the story, but I don't think the story begins with the wolf blowing down the second pig's house. Where does it begin?

STUDENT: With the three little pigs.

AMBASSADOR: Right. So can you show me that card?

STUDENT: [points to the card with the three little pigs]

AMBASSADOR: Great job! What do you see on that card?

STUDENT: The three little pigs.

AMBASSADOR: Great job! And what comes after that in the story?

STUDENT: [points to the second card]

AMBASSADOR: Great job! And what do you see on that card?

STUDENT: The big bad wolf.

AMBASSADOR: Great job! What happens next?

STUDENT: [points to the third card]

AMBASSADOR: Great job! What do you see there?

STUDENT: The big bad wolf says he's going to huff, and puff...

AMBASSADOR   ...*and blow the house down!*
AND STUDENT:

The Ambassador and student continue this process for the remainder of the cards in the story.

The Ambassador is asking the student to point to and explain each card in the story. Eventually, the student will begin to express what each card represents without needing to be prompted.

Because the end objective is to apply these skills to the events in a student's life, the Ambassador and student should think of an event in the student's life from that day. (Again, refer to our module **Passing the Baton** for related teaching points). Then the Ambassador and student should write down the events, using pictures, and repeat the exercise above with the events from the student's life.

Outro

The objective of this module was to help students with autism understand logical progressions through repetitions. These repetitions are especially important for a younger—or developmentally younger—student who might already be familiar with the story; the student must remember the events that are being represented instead of simply relying on her memory to help her place the cards in the correct order. As with all other modules, it is imperative that Ambassadors anticipate distracting situations that might arise and use their training to refocus the student's attention back on the task at hand. If necessary, it is fine for the Ambassador to improvise, as long as the improvisation falls well within the range of acceptable behavior. Should more assistance be necessary, the Ambassador should not hesitate to engage a teacher or school supervisor.

Passing the Baton

*An Autism Ambassadors
Original Module*

Intro

This module is geared toward teaching younger children how to use the all-important skill of make-believe storytelling while they are playing with friends, and how to go back and forth with friends while telling stories.

Telling stories, in the most basic sense, is a relatively simple thing to do; most people understand that a story has a beginning, a middle, and an end. If someone were to say, "I came home from school today and wanted to play baseball, but there was nobody outside to play with. So instead, I stayed indoors and played video games," that would fulfill the basic requirements for a story. There might be additional details (the storyteller might have mulled over going for a bike ride or watching a video) that either the storyteller or a friend could add to lend further intrigue or complexity to the story. However, for students with autism, basic storytelling structure is mystifying, and this usually leads to the student finding herself further isolated when it is time for storytelling or make-believe with her peers.

This module takes place in a lunch room in school; to replicate a lunch room setting, we need other students, which we will select from among the students in Ambassador training. All Ambassador trainees role-play and take turns being the student who needs assistance as well as other members of the class milling about. In addition, the Ambassador should provide a baton, or stick, or anything that can be passed back and forth to signify when it is the other person's turn to add storytelling details.

As with all of our other modules, should the student show signs of extended disengagement or display self-stimulatory behavior with her hands, the Ambassador should refer to our introductory module, **Pay Attention/Calm Hands,** in order to get the student to be fully present for the lesson.

We are now ready to begin. The Ambassador leads the student over to a lunch table, and they sit down.

AMBASSADOR: I have an idea—I'm in the mood to play make-believe. But not with toys or dolls. Let's tell a story together, okay?

STUDENT: How?

AMBASSADOR: First I'll tell part of the story; then you'll tell part of the story. Okay?

STUDENT: Okay.

AMBASSADOR: Okay, who do you want to tell a story about?

STUDENT: A girl named Miles.

> The student has made a small error, but one that the Ambassador can correct without much deviation from the exercise, as outlined below.

AMBASSADOR: Miles is a boy's name. Do you want to make him a boy?

STUDENT: Yes.

AMBASSADOR: Okay. So one day Miles decided to go to the playground. So he collected his playground toys, got on his bike, and what did he do next?

The Ambassador passes the baton to the student.

STUDENT: He took a bath.

> Relevance is one of the most challenging components of working with a student with autism. Because the hemispheres of their brains do not work well together, they frequently stray off topic, as exemplified above. The Ambassador needs to explain that, while it is possible for Miles to take a bath after getting on his bike, it is not what should happen next. We want this to continue to be a story about a boy who went to the playground on his bike. The Ambassador should give the student as many clues as possible about what the next point should involve.

The Ambassador gestures for the baton, which the student hands over to him.

AMBASSADOR: No. What does a bike do? Miles got on his bike and then he ...

The Ambassador passes the baton back to the student. (Note: This will now happen every time the story details are volleyed back and forth.)

STUDENT: ...rode his bike.

AMBASSADOR: Great job! And since he had his playground toys with him, where did he go on his bike?

STUDENT: He went to the playground.

AMBASSADOR: Great! So put those two things together: Miles ...

STUDENT: ...went to the playground on his bike.

> If the student has a hard time putting ideas together, the Ambassador should feel free to draw pictures on index cards, place them on the table, and let the student put the cards in the correct order. (See our module **Linear Sequencing** for further assistance on this topic.)

AMBASSADOR

Great job telling that part of the story!

> As with all of our other modules, when the student accomplishes something correctly, it is always a good idea for the Ambassador to compliment her, preferably by addressing exactly what the student did correctly (telling that part of the story). However, as the story progresses, the Ambassador should not feel impelled to compliment the student at every turn, as this might distract the student and interrupt her thinking process.

AMBASSADOR: Okay, so when Miles got to the playground, he went on the swings first. Then he wanted to run on the grass. What did the grass feel like?

STUDENT: It was wet.

> The Ambassador is asking the student to provide a jumping-off point. By asking the student to describe something rather than simply provide the next plot point, the Ambassador is giving the student the opportunity to branch off into more complicated storytelling and be a true collaborator.

AMBASSADOR: Great—tell me more about the grass.

STUDENT: It was green.

AMBASSADOR: I think you're right. But you also said it was wet. Why was it wet?

STUDENT: Because the sprinklers were on.

AMBASSADOR: Okay, since the sprinklers were on, Miles got his playground toys, went over to the sandbox, and . . .

STUDENT: . . . got on his bike.

AMBASSADOR: I don't think he got on his bike yet. I think he hadn't played with his playground toys yet, so since he was in the sandbox and wanted to play in the sand, he . . .

STUDENT: . . . played in the sandbox with his playground toys.

AMBASSADOR: You know what? I think that's exactly what he did!

> The Ambassador is building off of the student's plot point of Miles doing something else, but because the student went in a different direction, the Ambassador used the technique we detailed previously and led the student back to the logical flow of the story.

AMBASSADOR: And after he played in the sandbox, what do you think happened then?

STUDENT: He played some more!

AMBASSADOR: Right, but when he was done playing? What happened next?

STUDENT: He went home!

AMBASSADOR: How did he get home?

STUDENT: On his bike.

AMBASSADOR: Great job passing the baton!

> The basic beginning, middle, and end of the story have been established, so the Ambassador should signify this by complimenting the student.

> Once the student has generalized the basics of beginnings, middles, and ends, the Ambassador should work on expanding the student's critical thinking and collaborative storytelling abilities along the lines of what is outlined below.

AMBASSADOR: So let me ask you a question: Do you think Miles had fun today?

STUDENT: Yes.

AMBASSADOR: I do, too. Why do you think Miles had fun today?

STUDENT: Because he is a nice boy.

AMBASSADOR: I am sure Miles is a nice boy, too; I'll bet he has great playground toys and is a fun boy to play with. But why do you think he had fun today? What did he do today?

STUDENT:	He went to the playground.
AMBASSADOR:	Right. And is it fun to go to the playground?
STUDENT:	Yes.
AMBASSADOR:	So why did Miles have fun today?
STUDENT:	Because he went to the playground!
AMBASSADOR:	Good answer! What do we say when our story is finished?
STUDENT:	The End!

Outro

The objective of this module was to help the student create a clear beginning, middle, and end with assistance from the Ambassador. The student was able to make logical connections at every stage of the story and was therefore able to bring the story to a logical conclusion. If the student got sidetracked, the Ambassador guided her back to the story's logical progression without making the student feel self-conscious. Once the essential storytelling points had been laid down, the Ambassador was able to help the student add a critical thinking component to the story (do you think Miles enjoyed his day?), which will be especially helpful for older and/or more advanced students.

As with all other modules, it is imperative that Ambassadors anticipate distracting situations that might arise and use their training to refocus the student's attention back on the task at hand. If necessary, it is fine for the Ambassador to improvise, as long as the improvisation falls well within the range of acceptable behavior. Should more assistance be necessary, the Ambassador should not hesitate to engage a teacher or school supervisor.

Washing Hands at School

An Autism Ambassadors
Original Module

Intro

The goal of this module is to instruct Ambassadors in how to teach proper social etiquette to students with autism (especially younger students), so they can use these skills when they need to wash their hands in a school setting—and, ultimately, any other public setting.

Many students with autism have increased anxiety levels caused by external stimuli; everything from noises (even certain forms of otherwise pleasurable music) to lights or the feeling of someone's fingers on their skin can create distress for these students. Washing their hands, experiencing the feeling of water running over their skin, often falls squarely into this category. However, while certain noises or lights can often be avoided, hand-washing is a personal hygiene necessity that younger children need to be able to do without assistance from parents who will not be present during school hours. With repeated and incremental levels of desensitization, students with autism can overcome their sensitivity to the feeling of water and can therefore be depended upon to wash their hands several times throughout the day as part of their routines.

The module will take place in an actual school restroom, but preferably during a time when there are few or no others using it (e.g., before school, after school, or, if possible, during a free period). We will require other students to role-play everything from the student with autism to the occasional other student who comes in to use the bathroom facilities, so as to ensure as authentic an environment as possible.

As with all of our other modules, should the student show signs of extended disengagement or display self-stimulatory behavior with his hands, the Ambassador should refer to our introductory module **Pay Attention/Calm Hands** in order to get the student to be fully present for the lesson.

We are now ready to begin. The Ambassador and the student with autism enter the bathroom.

AMBASSADOR: (Student's name), we're about to go to lunch, so now we need to wash our hands.

STUDENT: [flaps hands]

The student likely knows that he is about to be getting his hands wet, so he may start to flap. While flapping is a typical stim, or nervous tic associated with students with autism, in this case the student might be attempting to busy his hands in order to keep them dry. Ambassadors should be ready to perform a counting exercise in order to quell the student's anxiety; if he still shows visible signs of anxiety, the Ambassador should dry her hands before taking the student's hands and placing them palms down on the table, gently but firmly, and repeating the following explanation as many times as necessary.

AMBASSADOR: (Student's name), whenever we are about to eat, or anytime after we use the bathroom, or anytime we get our hands dirty playing, we need to wash our hands. It's okay; water won't hurt you. We all drink water, we take a shower or bath in water, and we wash our hands with water.

The Ambassador is explaining the purpose of the exercise while simultaneously reassuring the student with things that are familiar to him.

AMBASSADOR: I know—before we wash our hands, let's play a game. Want to play a game?

STUDENT: [stops flapping]

AMBASSADOR: Great job!

As with all of our other modules, any time the student does something praiseworthy—in this case, calming himself down—the Ambassador should reward the student with praise.

AMBASSADOR: We're going to hold hands and count to three.

The Ambassador quickly runs her hands under the faucet, and then places her damp hands on top of the student's hands.

STUDENT: [whines, makes clucking sounds]

AMBASSADOR: Ready to count to three? One, two, three!

The Ambassador takes her hands away from the student's hands.

AMBASSADOR: Great job!

This is the first incremental stage in this module. Counting to three, which should be a familiar exercise to the student by now, helps the student focus on the end of the immediate task. It also helps to quell some of the frustration or fear the student is experiencing that comes from the Ambassador placing her wet hands on top of those of the student.

AMBASSADOR: Okay, let's play that game again. This time, however, let's count to ten.

STUDENT: [whines]

The Ambassador takes the student's hands and repeats the exercise, this time counting to ten before removing her hands from the student's.

STUDENT: [looks down; wipes his hands on his pants]

AMBASSADOR: Great job, but remember that we wipe our hands on paper towels, not our pants. There are lots of paper towels all over the bathroom.

The Ambassador points out the paper towels, taking a few from the dispenser and handing them to the student.

AMBASSADOR: Okay, now I'm going to wash my hands in the sink. First I'm going to run them under water.

The Ambassador puts her hands under the water in a hand washing movement (without soap) while counting to ten.

AMBASSADOR: Okay, I'm finished. Your turn!

At every turn in the exercise, especially during its most repetitive parts, the Ambassador's voice should be cheerful and upbeat, regardless of the student's responses (since the student will frequently voice his displeasure).

STUDENT: [places his hands under the water for ten seconds as the Ambassador counts out loud]

Should the student express a strong desire not to place his hands under the water, the Ambassador should go through the hand-washing motion while holding the student's hands. The Ambassador should do this while her hands are wet. Then the Ambassador should add water from the faucet while the student's hands are still being held by the Ambassador.

AMBASSADOR: Great job! Now let's add the soap.

STUDENT: No. My hands are clean now.

AMBASSADOR: Your hands are wet, but they're not clean. The soap cleans them. If we don't use soap, then all we did was make them wet for no reason. I'll go first.

> The soap is new, and its sliminess and/or suds might be disorienting or distracting to the student. Should the student resist the steps outlined below, the Ambassador should repeat the steps outlined above until the student is more relaxed.

The Ambassador squeezes out some liquid soap from the dispenser and rubs some on her hands, but does not rinse it off.

AMBASSADOR: Your turn!

The student takes some soap from the dispenser and rubs it on his hands, seemingly enjoying the sensation.

> The Ambassador might encounter the opposite problem here with the student, namely, that the student becomes accustomed to the sensation of soap on his hands and does not wish to wash it off. Should that be the case, the Ambassador should allow the student to wash it off, little by little, using the same counting exercise as outlined above.

AMBASSADOR: Okay, now we're going to wash off the soap. My turn first.

The Ambassador washes off the soap, removes a paper towel from the dispenser, and dries her hands on the paper towel.

AMBASSADOR: Your turn!

STUDENT: [rinses off his hands]

AMBASSADOR: Great job! Now dry your hands!

STUDENT: [goes to dry his hands on his pants again]

AMBASSADOR: Paper towel, remember?

STUDENT: [removes a paper towel from the dispenser and dries his hands on the towel]

AMBASSADOR: Great job washing your hands!

Outro

In order to overcome the fear and anxiety caused by getting wet, the Ambassador used several smaller, incremental steps that resulted in the student becoming increasingly more comfortable with the notion of wetting his hands. By making sure the student was comfortable with each step before moving on, the Ambassador worked toward decreasing the student's anxiety when his hands were wet. These types of incremental steps can also be worked beyond this exercise until the student is able to comfortably spend time in the water at a pool or at the beach with his friends. (Added steps should be taken to include the student's feet as well.)

As with all other modules, it is imperative that Ambassadors anticipate distracting situations that might arise and use their training to refocus the student's attention back on the task at hand. If necessary, it is fine for the Ambassador to improvise, as long as the improvisation falls well within the range of acceptable behavior. Should more assistance be necessary, the Ambassador should not hesitate to engage a teacher or school supervisor.

Academic/ In-Class Modules

You might have noticed by now that much of our curriculum is based in education-based behavior modification rather than in formal classroom instruction. Autism Ambassadors is, however, a school-related curriculum, and so this category is our largest one, although only a few of our modules pertain to the student's actual academic work. The rest of these modules address the need for the student to be able to function in the classroom and to integrate herself into her academic environment as seamlessly as possible. This is extremely important, because one of Autism Ambassadors' principal objectives is to provide extra assistance to teachers so they can focus on other classroom resources; if our programs are not generalized by the students for whom they are intended, then our program is not making good on one of its most important promises.

The ten modules that make up this category are as follows:

1. Raise Your Hand

2. Asserting Yourself in Class

3. Taking Notes

4. Giving an Oral Report in Class

5. Replacing Classroom Items

6. Switching Desks

7. Watching a Video in Class

8. Writing an Intro Paragraph

9. Writing a Chunk Paragraph

10. Writing a Concluding Paragraph

Raise Your Hand teaches the student when and when not to raise her hand. After all, it is one thing to teach a student to raise her hand when she knows the answer to a question; it is another thing entirely to teach that student when it is appropriate to keep her hand down, even if she knows the answer to a question (which, in the example in this module, involves another student asking if he can use the bathroom). This module teaches discretion and decision making, which are building blocks for students with autism that will carry over into other classroom-related skill set areas as well.

Asserting Yourself in Class, which should be taught in conjunction with our **Raise Your Hand** module, reinforces the skills involved in teaching a student when and when not to raise his hand, but it adds a social component in that it also teaches the student how to channel his anxiety in ways that ensure a productive result. This module builds confidence, as it teaches students with autism to assert their views; they learn to view themselves as constructive participants in the classroom who can offer their opinions on anything the teacher is covering in class that day.

Taking Notes addresses a seemingly basic skill—writing down what the teacher says in class—that is far more complicated than it sounds. Just as we learned in our **Raise Your Hand** module, making distinctions between when and when not to act can be extremely difficult for students with autism. In this case, teaching students with autism what to and what not to write down reinforces the difference between note taking and unfiltered transcription, which, left to their own devices (and given the predisposition and affinity of many of them toward detail gathering) they will more likely than not opt for.

Giving an Oral Report in Class broaches the multifaceted issues students with autism frequently have with anxiety and gives the students a skill set that not only helps them overcome their fears but also enables them to organize their thoughts into a logical, cogent presentation that the class and teacher can enjoy. This module can be taught in conjunction with our **Logical Sequencing** module from our **Younger/Lower Functioning Students** category, as both modules address the organizational and structural principles involved in critical thinking.

Replacing Classroom Items teaches students with autism how to remain calm when familiar objects in the classroom are moved or displaced for any one of a variety of reasons. Familiarity and order are crucial in the minds of students with autism, and their anxiety tends to rise when object placements to which they have grown accustomed are moved elsewhere, as frequently needs to be the case in classrooms. This module works a number of desensitization exercises (including counting, a staple of ABA-based training) into the student's approach to upheaval, even upheaval as seemingly minor as one president's portrait being replaced by that of another.

Switching Desks is a module in the vein of **Replacing Classroom Items**; it is our recommendation that the two be taught in tandem. Because students move their desks at times during the year, either to gain a better vantage point to the teacher or simply for the purposes of forming clusters for a group project, this is an important exercise to teach self-regulation to students with autism in a constantly changing environment, similar to the exercise above.

Watching a Video in Class is another module that teaches a skill that sounds far easier than it is. Though it might seem like a piece of cake to watch an educational (or even entertaining) video in class, students with autism frequently experience anxiety when the lights go down and they are left in the dark to watch something with which they are not familiar. In this exercise Ambassadors teach desensitization and redirection to ensure a positive experience for the student with autism, and by extension, for all of her classmates as well.

Writing an Intro Paragraph is a skill that is being taught in most schools using the cone structure: General subject matter is discussed first, and then more specific material follows; culminating in the essay's thesis statement. Ambassadors should feel free to use an actual sno-cone (or paper mache cone, if the icy variety is not feasible) as a visual aid, along with a whiteboard and marker to supplement their lesson objectives as they walk through the exercise. This module is taught in conjunction with **Writing a Chunk Paragraph** and **Writing a Concluding Paragraph**, as the Ambassador and student will work with one essay prompt and follow it all the way through to its completion.

Writing a Chunk Paragraph teaches students how to use a basic topic sentence idea (the chunk) and support it with two details. Ambassadors are encouraged to use a brownie in order to symbolize the idea, using the chocolate chips in the brownie to serve as symbols for the supporting details. Should the student have dietary restrictions, as many students with autism do (many students with autism are on a gluten/casein-free diet), the Ambassador should substitute different colors and varieties of Play-Doh or some other modeling clay. The paragraph itself will be a continuation from the introductory paragraph established in the module above.

Writing a Concluding Paragraph is a skill that is being taught in most schools using a pyramid structure: Specific subject matter is discussed first, and then increasingly general material follows leading to a concluding statement, building on the concept of a concluding thought that was established in the chunk paragraph module. Ambassadors use an actual toy Egyptian pyramid of the variety used in classrooms (or a paper mache version if they cannot obtain a pretend Egyptian pyramid) as a visual aid along with a whiteboard and marker.

Raise Your Hand

An Autism Ambassadors
Original Module

Intro

The purpose of this lesson is to teach students with autism how to interact appropriately by raising their hands when they wish to participate in the class lesson. Students with autism tend to either speak out of turn or not at all; this module will teach them how to find the happy medium where they feel comfortable participating when they know the answer to questions, as well as whenever general participation from all students is required. This module will build confidence on the part of students with autism and will make them feel more integrated into the classroom environment, which will in turn enable them to learn more in their academic endeavors.

This module takes place at the student's desk in school. Schools will often assign a specific desk to each student. To simulate this situation, you can use a sharpie to mark a letter or a number on a piece of paper and then tape it on the desk or chair you use in the module. In our exercise, we have put a felt *A* on the desk where we want the student to sit. To replicate a classroom setting, we need other students, which we will select from among the students in Ambassador training. All Ambassador trainees role-play and take turns being the student with autism. The student simulators will sit at desks near the student with autism, while another student will sit in a teacher's chair.

As with all of our other modules, should the student show signs of extended disengagement or display self-stimulatory behavior with her hands, the Ambassador should refer to our introductory module **Pay Attention/Calm Hands** in order to get the student to be fully present for the lesson.

We are now ready to begin.

AMBASSADOR playing the TEACHER:	Good morning, class. Today we are going to study the American Revolution.

Since we are teaching students with autism to raise their hands during appropriate times in teacher's lessons, and since those lessons can vary depending on the subject being discussed, we will teach students how to raise their hands not only at times when they wish to contribute, but also at other times when they are being asked simply to participate along with the rest of the group.

STUDENT:	[sits playing with her hands]
TEACHER:	We are going to start by discussing the father of our country. Who here knows who the father of our country was?
STUDENT:	[squirms in her seat]
TEACHER:	Anyone who knows the answer, please raise your hand.
STUDENT:	[Flaps hands, continues to squirm in her seat]
TEACHER:	(Student's name), would you like to answer the question?
STUDENT:	I don't know.
TEACHER:	Do you know the answer to the question?
STUDENT:	No.

Students with autism will frequently manifest signs of anxiety when asked to participate in public or social settings. While the student might not know the answer to many of the questions being asked, the Ambassador should make sure to use questions that he knows the student can answer.

AMBASSADOR:	[leaning over to student] (Student's name), didn't we just read about this in our homework?
STUDENT:	[nods her head]
AMBASSADOR:	Great! And do you remember reading about who the father of our country was?
STUDENT:	Yes.
AMBASSADOR:	Great! Then you do know the answer to the teacher's question! So raise your hand if you want to answer the question.
STUDENT:	[flaps hands, squirms in her seat again]
AMBASSADOR:	(Student's name), if you know the answer to the question, please let me know that by raising your hand. That's your way of telling me that you know the answer to the question and want to answer the question.

Since many students with autism flap their hands, it is important to emphasize the redirection of the student's hand from flapping to being raised proudly in the air. Additionally, the Ambassador should continue to repeat the prompt in its entirety to enable the student with autism to stay on task.

STUDENT: Looks uncomfortable.

AMBASSADOR: What's wrong?

STUDENT: I don't want to answer the question.

AMBASSADOR: It's always a good idea to answer questions in class; you'll earn the respect of your teachers and the other students, but you can't do that unless you raise your hand first to let the teacher know that you know the answer.

As with other modules, it is always a good idea for the Ambassador to explain why the student with autism should want to participate in the exercise. Nothing should be taken for granted when it comes to motivating the student.

STUDENT: [raises her hand]

TEACHER: Good raising your hand, (student's name). Would you like to answer the question?

STUDENT: I don't know.

TEACHER: Would you like me to repeat the question?

STUDENT: Nods her head.

TEACHER: Okay. The question was, who was the father of our country?

STUDENT: George Washington was the father of our country.

TEACHER: Correct! Good answer! George Washington was the father of our country. Now when he crossed....

STUDENT: [raises her hand again]

TEACHER: It's not time to raise your hand yet, because I haven't asked a question. Please wait until I ask a question.

STUDENT: Okay.

TEACHER: Now when George Washington crossed the Delaware, that was a major turning point in the American Revolution.

[teacher pauses, and then asks]

TEACHER: Now who wants to go to lunch?

AMBASSADOR: (Student's name), that's another question, but it's not one you have to answer; all you have to do is raise your hand if you want to go to lunch.

[All the students, including the student with autism, raise their hands.]

Outro

For this lesson we taught our Ambassadors how to encourage the student with autism to understand when it was appropriate to raise her hand. We made a distinction between questions that required the hand-raising to be followed up with an answer, and questions that simply required the student to raise her hand. As we mentioned in the learning moments, this will not come easily to the assigned students, nor will it come easily to the Ambassadors. However, Ambassadors should continue to simulate every kind of question-answering opportunity they can think of, using the exercises outlined above.

As with all other modules, it is imperative that Ambassadors anticipate distracting situations that might arise and use their training to refocus the student with autism's attention back on the task at hand. If necessary, it is fine for the Ambassador to improvise, as long as the improvisation falls well within the range of acceptable behavior. Should more assistance be necessary, the Ambassador should not hesitate to engage a teacher or school supervisor.

Asserting Yourself in Class

An Autism Ambassadors
Original Module

Intro

The purpose of this module is to teach students with autism how to interact appropriately when they need to assert their ideas, ask questions, or otherwise make themselves heard in their classes.

Students with autism tend to either speak out of turn or not at all. For them, the back and forth of teacher instruction followed by questions from the class is confusing and alienating. This module will teach these students how to find the happy medium where they feel comfortable participating not only when they do not understand something in class but also when they know the answers to questions and wish to answer them. Additionally, they will be taught how to assert themselves should they need to use the restroom or if another student is bothering them. In this regard, this module extends upon skills taught in our other module **Raise Your Hand,** which should be taught in conjunction with this module.

This module takes place at the student's desk in school. Schools will often assign a specific desk to each student. To simulate this situation, you can use a sharpie to mark a letter or a number on a piece of paper and then tape it on the desk or chair. In our exercise, we have put a felt *A* on the desk where we want the student to sit. To replicate a classroom setting, we need other students, which we will select from among the students in Ambassador training. All Ambassador trainees role-play and take turns being the student with autism. The student simulators will sit at desks near the student with autism, while another student will sit in a teacher's chair and play the teacher.

As with all of our other modules, should the student show signs of extended disengagement or display self-stimulatory behavior with his hands, the Ambassador should refer to our introductory module **Pay Attention/Calm Hands** in order to get the student to be fully present for the lesson.

We are now ready to begin. The Ambassador and the student with autism enter the classroom and take their seats.

AMBASSADOR: (Student's name), today we are going to learn how to make ourselves heard in class.

STUDENT: [stares straight ahead]

AMBASSADOR: What that means is that we are going to learn not only how to answer the teacher but also to ask her when we have a question about what she's teaching or to use the bathroom.

> Even if the student is not responding, it is always a good idea for the Ambassador to explain everything she is going to introduce in the course of the module.

The teacher enters and walks over to the teacher's desk.

AMBASSADOR
playing the
TEACHER: Good morning, class. Today we are going to study the American Revolution.

> Since we are teaching students with autism to raise their hands during appropriate times in teachers' lessons, and since those lessons can vary depending on the subject being discussed, at this point please refer to our previous **Raise Your Hand** module to teach students how to raise their hands.

STUDENT: [sits playing with, or flapping, his hands; stares away from the teacher]

AMBASSADOR: (Student's name), please look at the teacher.

STUDENT: [turns to face the teacher]

> Since the student was told at the beginning of the lesson that he was going to be expected to ask a question, he might be experiencing a fair amount of anxiety and, as a result, might be less cooperative than usual. Ambassadors should anticipate this and be ready to call upon basic autism training skills like teaching students to pay attention.

TEACHER: We are going to start with a discussion about one of the most important events of the American Revolution: George Washington's crossing of the Delaware.

STUDENT:	[squirms in his seat]
AMBASSADOR:	[leans over and prompts] (Student's name), do you know what the Delaware is?
STUDENT:	No.
AMBASSADOR:	Do you want to ask the teacher what the Delaware is?
STUDENT:	[nods]
AMBASSADOR:	Great! Raise your hand.
STUDENT:	[flaps hands, squirms in his seat again]
AMBASSADOR:	(Student's name), if you raise your hand, that's your way of telling your teacher that you have a question.

> Since many students with autism flap their hands, it is important to emphasize the redirection of the student's hand from flapping to being raised in the air.

> It is important to distinguish between raising a hand to answer a question and raising a hand to ask a question. The Ambassador and teacher should alternate between the former and the latter following the formal end of this exercise, just to make the distinction clear.

STUDENT:	[raises his hand halfway, tentatively]
AMBASSADOR:	Good raising your hand, but raise it high in the air so the teacher can see. That way, the teacher will know that you want to ask a question.
TEACHER:	(Student's name), would you like to ask a question?
STUDENT:	Yes.

> The student might get confused or disoriented at this point and think that his obligation is finished. The Ambassador should be ready to intervene and remind the student to ask his question.

AMBASSADOR:	(Student's name), what was your question?
STUDENT:	What is the Delaware?
TEACHER:	Great question! Delaware is the name of a state, but it is also the name of a river that George Washington crossed with his troops, which positioned them to attack the British. Now, do you know who George Washington was?
STUDENT:	[nods]

TEACHER:	Would you like to tell me who George Washington was?
AMBASSADOR:	
STUDENT:	[nods again]
AMBASSADOR:	Great—raise your hand.
STUDENT:	[raises his hand]
TEACHER:	(Student's name), who was George Washington?
STUDENT:	The father of our country.
TEACHER:	Great answer!
AMBASSADOR:	(Student's name), do you need to use the restroom?
STUDENT:	Yes.

> Should the student say "no," the Ambassador should raise her own hand and ask the teacher to use the restroom so the student watches the process.

AMBASSADOR:	Raise your hand and ask the teacher.
STUDENT:	[raises his hand]
TEACHER:	Yes, (student's name)?
STUDENT:	Can I use the restroom?
TEACHER:	Yes. Good job asserting yourself!

Outro

In this module, we taught our Ambassadors how to encourage students with autism when it is appropriate to raise their hands to assert themselves. As we mentioned in the learning moments, it is important to make distinctions between when it is appropriate for students with autism to *ask* questions, and how these students should go about *answering* questions in class. Once the basic skills of this module have been mastered, they should be applied toward every other academic subject—Math, English, et cetera—until the student understands not only how to assert himself, but how to do so repeatedly under all circumstances.

Note that, like a typical student, a student with autism might have inherent difficulty with a subject; it should be emphasized by the Ambassador that this is completely normal, and the Ambassador should make a point of discussing her own academic difficulties with the student with autism so the student does not feel an added element of inhibition in addition to his natural autism-related issues.

As with all other modules, it is imperative that Ambassadors anticipate distracting situations that might arise and use their training to refocus the student's attention back on the task at hand. If necessary, it is fine for the Ambassador to improvise, as long as the improvisation falls well within the range of acceptable behavior. Should more assistance be necessary, the Ambassador should not hesitate to engage a teacher or school supervisor.

Taking Notes
in Class

*An Autism Ambassadors
Original Module*

Intro

The purpose of this module is to teach students with autism how to take notes appropriately and comprehensively in class. It takes place at the student's desk in school. Schools will often assign a specific desk to each student. To simulate this situation, you can use a sharpie to mark a letter or a number on a piece of paper and then tape it on the desk or chair. In our exercise, we have put a felt *A* on the desk where we want the student to sit. To replicate a classroom setting, we need other students, which we will select from among the students in Ambassador training. All Ambassador trainees role-play and take turns being the student with autism. Student simulators will sit at desks near the student with autism, while another student will sit in a teacher's chair. The Ambassador should be seated right next to the student with autism so that the Ambassador can help guide and oversee all of the student's note-taking.

As with all of our other modules, should the student show signs of extended disengagement or display self-stimulatory behavior with her hands, the Ambassador should refer to our introductory module **Pay Attention/Calm Hands** in order to get the student to be fully present for the lesson.

We are now ready to begin.

AMBASSADOR playing the TEACHER:	Good morning, class. Today we are going to study the American Revolution.

[The students take out their notebooks, except the student with autism, who stares at the teacher.]

AMBASSADOR: (Student's name), the teacher is going to teach us a lesson about the American Revolution. That means you need to take out your notebook and write down notes. Notes are short words that explain to us what the teacher is talking about.

STUDENT: [stares out the window, fidgets, plays with her pencil]

> Students with autism, even those who are able to function in mainstream classrooms, frequently experience problems paying attention in class. Ambassadors need to be especially cognizant of this, especially for the purposes of this exercise, which can be extremely useful in helping students stay on task.

AMBASSADOR: Here, let me help you. First, take out your notebook and a pencil.

STUDENT: [takes out notebook and pencil]

AMBASSADOR: Now listen for important facts and write them down.

STUDENT: Why?

AMBASSADOR: Because later, when we have to study for a test, you will have the important facts right in front of you. Otherwise, if you don't write them down, you might forget them, and then when it comes time to take the test, you won't do well on the test.

> Even if the student doesn't ask why she should take notes, it is a good idea for the Ambassador to explain the reasoning behind this step. Very little should be taken for granted when it comes to these students' cognitive reasoning abilities, and Ambassadors should always err on the side of caution.

TEACHER: In 1776, Thomas Jefferson wrote the Declaration of Independence. It was signed on July 4th, 1776.

AMBASSADOR: (Student's name), do you want to write those facts down?

STUDENT: Why?

AMBASSADOR: Well, because we're studying the American Revolution. The Declaration of Independence was one of the most important parts of the American Revolution, and the date it was signed and who wrote it are both important facts, too, right?

STUDENT: Right.

AMBASSADOR: Great. So what do you want to write down first?

STUDENT: Did I write the Declaration of Independence?

AMBASSADOR: No, (student's name). Thomas Jefferson wrote the Declaration of Independence. You wrote a note about Thomas Jefferson writing the Declaration of Independence.

> Because the Ambassador has prompted the student to write and the teacher also used that word, the student is experiencing some confusion. Ambassadors need to exercise caution when choosing their words, and should the student fuse two ideas together, the Ambassador should be ready to explain the difference between what the student is doing and what the student is writing about.

STUDENT: [writes that Thomas Jefferson wrote the Declaration of Independence]

AMBASSADOR: Great. What do you want to write down next?

STUDENT: Thomas Jefferson wrote the Declaration of Independence.

AMBASSADOR: Right. That's who. But when was it signed?

STUDENT: July 4, 1776.

AMBASSADOR: Great job! Now write down that the Declaration of Independence was signed on July 4th, 1776.

A classmate raises his hand.

TEACHER: Yes, (Name of classmate raising hand)?

CLASSMATE: May I please go to the bathroom?

TEACHER: Yes, you may.

STUDENT: [starts writing that classmate went to bathroom]

AMBASSADOR: (Student's name), the teacher and (classmate's name) were only talking about going to the bathroom.

STUDENT: But he raised his hand, and the teacher said that he could go to the bathroom.

AMBASSADOR: I know, but we only write down important notes about American history. Since the bathroom isn't the same as American history, we don't have to write that down.

> As this interchange illustrates, students with autism might need help to determine what is and is not relevant to the note-taking process. The Ambassador needs to anticipate this and be ready to help the student understand what warrants being written down and what doesn't.

TEACHER: The Declaration of Independence was America's way of announcing that it was no longer part of the British Empire.

STUDENT:　　　[writes this down]

AMBASSADOR:　　Good job taking notes!

As with all of our modules, whenever a student with autism does something correctly, the Ambassador should positively reinforce that action.

Outro

In this module, we taught a series of steps that began with preparation—taking out notebooks, pencils, and any other pertinent materials—and then progressed to basic note-taking skills. We also established when it is and is not appropriate to take notes, as exemplified with the student who raised his hand to go to the bathroom.

As with all other modules, it is imperative that Ambassadors anticipate distracting situations that might arise and use their training to refocus the student with autism's attention back on the task at hand. If necessary, it is fine for the Ambassador to improvise, as long as the improvisation falls well within the range of acceptable behavior. Should more assistance be necessary, the Ambassador should not hesitate to engage a teacher or school supervisor.

Giving an Oral Report in Class

An Autism Ambassadors
Original Module

Intro

The objective of this module is to help students with autism give oral presentations in class in a logical manner that is easy for others to follow. Many people have difficulty telling a story's events in linear order; even a number of adults find themselves, during dinner conversations, saying things like "Oh, I forgot to mention. . . ." or "Remind me: Did I already say the part where I . . . ?" and even when they fail to include important story-telling details, they can be made aware of this by a listening party.

Students with autism, however, have a much harder time relating details in order than do typical students. In addition, consider this statistic: When polled, people consistently say that their number one fear is speaking in public; year in, year out, this fear beats out visits to the dentist and even death. Now consider the fact that not only do students with autism have to overcome a devastating disability in order to tell a series of events in logical, sequential order, they also must overcome the already considerable anxiety they feel whenever called upon to do anything that involves social behavior, and they must do so in front of a classroom filled with their peers.

This module takes place in a classroom in school; to replicate a classroom setting, we need other students, which we will select from among the students in Ambassador training. All Ambassador trainees role-play and take turns being the student who needs assistance as well as other members of the class milling about.

As with all of our other modules, should the student show signs of extended disengagement or display self-stimulatory behavior with his hands, the Ambassador should refer to our introductory module **Pay Attention/Calm Hands** in order to get the student to be fully present for the lesson.

We are now ready to begin. The Ambassador and the student with autism sit at a desk in the classroom.

AMBASSADOR: (Student's name), today we are going to do oral reports. That means that we are going to talk about something that is important to us, but we are going to do it in front of the entire class.

STUDENT: [looks away; seems nervous]

AMBASSADOR: I know it sounds scary. We are all scared when we have to speak in public. Every one of your classmates is nervous about giving his report.

> Validating the student's concerns by highlighting those of the rest of the class is a good way to ease him into the exercise. Students with autism are frequently aware of their outsider status, and the more the student feels as though he is in sync with the rest of the class, the less likely he is to resist.

AMBASSADOR: First we're going to prepare for our essay. I'm going to do my essay on the movie *Avatar*. What would you like to talk about for your essay?

STUDENT: Kobe Bryant.

> For the purposes of this exercise, the oral report need not be on something academic. Allowing the student to pick a subject of his liking is an excellent way to get the student engaged and motivated and will likely lead to a more successful outcome.

AMBASSADOR: Okay, great! First we're going to plan our speeches. That's called an outline. What is the first thing you want to say about Kobe Bryant?

> The Ambassador should be writing all of the student's key bullet points down, which she will use as something of a crib sheet for when the student and Ambassador are comparing notes after the speech.

STUDENT: I don't know him.

> The student does not supply an appropriate thesis statement here. A student might very well answer the Ambassador's prompt with something even more off topic, like "I like chess" or "The Mavericks are my favorite team." (Kobe Bryant plays for the Lakers.) As is the case in all of our other modules, the Ambassador needs to gently steer the student back on track, but also needs to prompt with something that will lead the student toward supplying a viable thesis statement for his report.

AMBASSADOR: I don't know Kobe Bryant either, but perhaps we can get to know him better if we learn a little bit more about him. What can you tell me about Kobe Bryant?

STUDENT: He plays basketball.

AMBASSADOR: Great job! Write that down. What team does he play for?

STUDENT: The Lakers.

AMBASSADOR: Great job! Write that down. And why do you want to talk about Kobe Bryant today?

The Ambassador now switches from "what" questions to "why" questions, shifting the emphasis off of detail questions and on to more critical thinking questions. Together, the Ambassador and student can now explore correlations between basic information and why that information is important.

The Ambassador should always be reminding the student to write down anything the Ambassador feels will be suitable for the student's outline.

STUDENT: Because he's my favorite player.

AMBASSADOR: And why is he your favorite player?

STUDENT: Because he's really good.

AMBASSADOR: And what makes him really good?

STUDENT: He scores a lot of points.

AMBASSADOR: And what is the result of him scoring a lot of points? Do the Lakers win or lose?

STUDENT: Win.

AMBASSADOR: Win what?

STUDENT: The championship!

It is important for the Ambassador to lead the student to a point of conclusion; without understanding where the essay is going, the student will likely continue to supply detail after detail. This is no different for reports in which the student is discussing a movie or a political event; the movie has to end, and the event has to come to some resolution. Having an end objective to the speech gives the speech necessary structure. (See our modules **Logical Sequencing** and **Passing the Baton** for further thoughts on this part of the process.)

AMBASSADOR: Great report! Now let's see what you wrote down.

> The Ambassador looks at the student's notes, comparing them with her own and helping to organize them if need be.

AMBASSADOR: Great job! Now let's stand in front of the class and talk about Kobe Bryant.

STUDENT: [whines]

AMBASSADOR: You don't have to talk about everything we just did, in the order we just did it. You can just talk however you want.

> The Ambassador is trying to desensitize the student to the idea of speaking in public by allowing him to stand in front of the class and pretty much speak freestyle. The Ambassador should time the student for roughly two minutes and not worry if the student strays off topic.

The student stands up and walks up to the front of the classroom and starts to speak. When two minutes are up, the Ambassador and the other students clap.

AMBASSADOR: Great job! Now it's time to give your speech!

STUDENT: [flaps hands]

AMBASSADOR: I understand you're nervous. But remember, so is everyone else. And look! You've got your whole speech right in front of you in the outline! You can look down at your outline as often as you like.

> The Ambassador should not only reiterate the everyone's-in-the-same-boat argument but should also try to reassure the student by reminding him that the speech has already been written.

The student stands up and walks up to the front of the classroom and starts to speak. The Ambassador, culling from her own notes, gently prompts the student if he strays too far off topic. The student finishes and the class applauds.

AMBASSADOR: Great speech! You did it!

Outro

The goal of this module is to desensitize students to the idea of public speaking by giving them a topic they enjoy discussing, and then teaching them how to write an outline. Once students are more comfortable with the topic, they are able to add the public speaking component to the exercise. As with all other modules, it is imperative that Ambassadors anticipate distracting situations that might arise and use their training to refocus the student's attention back on the task at hand. If necessary, it is fine for the Ambassador to improvise, as long as the improvisation falls well within the range of acceptable behavior. Should more assistance be necessary, the Ambassador should not hesitate to engage a teacher or school supervisor.

Replacing
Classroom Items

An Autism Ambassadors
Original Module

Intro

The purpose of this module is to help students with autism react appropriately to the multitude of changes to their routines that they might face on a daily basis. Many students with autism depend on things and places that are very familiar, as familiarity and routine are frequently sources of comfort for them and help quell their anxieties. However, in the course of an average school day, there is considerable potential for disruption to these students' routines, and the reaction of students with autism to these disruptions can create chaos and distraction for other students.

This module takes place at the student's desk in school. Schools will often assign a specific desk to each student. To simulate this situation, you can use a sharpie to mark a letter or a number on a piece of paper and then tape it on the desk or chair. We have put a felt *A* on the desk where we want the student to sit. To replicate a classroom setting, we need other students, which we will select from among the students in Ambassador training. All Ambassador trainees role-play and take turns being the student with autism. The student simulators will sit at desks near the student with autism, while another student will sit in a teacher's chair and play the teacher.

Note that there is another lesson with which this lesson should be paired called **Switching Desks.**

In this lesson we will address issues that involve helping the student with autism be flexible when it comes to an object in the classroom being moved. In **Switching Desks,** we will address what happens when the location of a student's desk is changed (as is often the case in middle school), or another student wishes to sit in a seat familiar to that of the student with autism (as is often the case in high school).

As with all of our other modules, should the student show signs of extended disengagement or display self-stimulatory behavior with her hands, the Ambassador should refer to our introductory module **Pay**

Attention/Calm Hands in order to get the student to be fully present for the lesson.

We are now ready to begin. The student with autism enters the classroom and sits down at her desk.

AMBASSADOR playing the TEACHER:	Good morning, class. We are moving on to a new lesson today, so since we are no longer studying George Washington, I am going to replace his poster with a John Adams poster. We will be studying him next. [teacher takes down the George Washington poster]
STUDENT:	[flaps hands]
AMBASSADOR:	What's wrong, (student's name)?
STUDENT:	[continues to flap hands]
AMBASSADOR:	Use your words. Tell me what's wrong.
STUDENT:	Poster.

> The Ambassador needs to understand that, while no disruption is a good idea, language is always preferable to physical gestures. Asking a student to use her words is the first step toward achieving socially acceptable behavior.

TEACHER:	[puts the George Washington poster back in its place, waits for five seconds, then takes the poster down again]
STUDENT:	[starts to flap hands again]
AMBASSADOR:	Use your words.
STUDENT:	Poster.
TEACHER:	[replaces the George Washington poster with a poster of John Adams]
STUDENT:	Poster.

> Should the student revert to flapping or any other form of nonverbal expression, the Ambassador should remind the student to use her words as many times as necessary.

AMBASSADOR:	(Student's name), the teacher put a poster up.
STUDENT:	Poster! Poster!
AMBASSADOR:	The teacher put up a poster of John Adams because we are no longer studying George Washington.

The Ambassador needs to explain to the student that, while this isn't exactly what the student wanted, it is a half-step. The goal is to get the student to become accustomed to the change, in gradual stages, until the student is no longer agitated.

STUDENT: [whines]

AMBASSADOR: I know—let's count to ten.

STUDENT: [counts to ten]

AMBASSADOR: Good counting!

Counting is frequently used as a coping mechanism for students with autism. Ambassadors can teach students in these situations to count in order to offset their anxiety, although Ambassadors should emphasize that students need to count softly so as not to disrupt the class.

Even though it might seem inconsequential, the Ambassador should compliment the student for successfully counting to ten, because it reinforces the positive choice the student has made in assuaging her anxiety.

The teacher replaces the John Adams poster with the George Washington poster. The teacher waits five seconds again, then takes down the George Washington poster and replaces it with the John Adams poster.

STUDENT: [whines]

AMBASSADOR: Use your words.

STUDENT: Poster.

AMBASSADOR: We're not studying George Washington anymore; we're studying John Adams. So we need to put up a poster of John Adams.

The Ambassador needs to repeat the reason behind the switching of the poster, even though he just mentioned it a minute or two ago. He should never underestimate the level of anxiety that can come about as a result of changes in the routines of these students.

AMBASSADOR: Let's count to five this time.

> Little by little, the Ambassador should try to ease the student away from having to count at all. Thus we start with a ten-count, then reduce it to a five-count, et cetera.

STUDENT:	[counts to five]
AMBASSADOR:	Good job counting!
TEACHER:	[stands by the John Adams poster, but makes no further moves to replace it] John Adams was our country's second president....
STUDENT:	[flaps] Poster.
TEACHER:	[continues teaching] He succeeded George Washington....
STUDENT:	[counts to ten, then counts to five, then is quiet]
AMBASSADOR:	(Student's name), great job being quiet!

Outro

The objective of this module was to teach students with autism how to calm themselves down when familiar classroom items are replaced. We began by replacing the item in stages and taught the student how to regulate her response accordingly. This lesson can be repeated with everything from a globe to a pet cage and should be done incrementally until the student puts up little to no resistance to the classroom item being moved. As with all other modules, it is imperative that Ambassadors anticipate distracting situations that might arise and use their training to refocus the student's attention back on the task at hand. If necessary, it is fine for the Ambassador to improvise, as long as the improvisation falls well within the range of acceptable behavior. Should more assistance be necessary, the Ambassador should not hesitate to engage a teacher or school supervisor.

Switching Desks

*An Autism Ambassadors
Original Module*

Intro

The purpose of this module is to help students with autism react appropriately to the multitude of changes to their routines that they might face on a daily basis. Many students with autism depend on things and places that are very familiar, as familiarity and routine are frequently sources of comfort for them and help quell their anxieties. However, in the course of an average school day, there is considerable potential for disruption to these students' routines, and the reaction of students with autism to these disruptions can create chaos and distraction for other students.

This module takes place at the student's desk in school. Schools will often assign a specific desk to each student. To simulate this situation, you can use a sharpie to mark a letter or a number on a piece of paper and then tape it on the desk or chair. In our exercise, we have put a felt *A* on the desk where we want the student to sit. To replicate a classroom setting, we need other students, which we will select from among the students in Ambassador training. All Ambassador trainees role-play and take turns being the student with autism. The student simulators sit at desks near the student with autism.

Note that there is another lesson with which this lesson should be paired, called **Replacing Classroom Items.** In this lesson we will address issues that involve helping the student with autism be flexible when it comes to his desk being moved. In **Replacing Classroom Items,** we address what happens when a standard classroom item, such as a globe or wall poster, is moved.

As with all of our other modules, should the student show signs of extended disengagement or display self-stimulatory behavior with his hands, the Ambassador should refer to our introductory module **Pay Attention/Calm Hands** in order to get the student to be fully present for the lesson.

We are now ready to begin. The student with autism enters the classroom and sits down at his desk, and the Ambassador playing the teacher stands at the front of the room.

AMBASSADOR playing the TEACHER:	Good morning, class. Since we have been sitting in the same desks for a month now, it's time to switch. (Student with autism's name), why don't you switch with (another student's name)?

The other student gets up and walks over to the student with autism, who flaps his hands.

AMBASSADOR:	What's wrong, (student's name)?
STUDENT:	[continues to flap hands]
AMBASSADOR:	Use your words. Tell me what's wrong.
STUDENT:	I don't want to move.

> The Ambassador needs to understand that, while no disruption is a good idea, language is always preferable to physical gestures. Asking a student to use his words is the first step toward achieving socially acceptable behavior.

AMBASSADOR:	We need to switch desks every month so that every student gets a chance to sit in every part of the classroom.
STUDENT:	Why?
AMBASSADOR:	Well, why do you think?
STUDENT:	They like my desk better.

> Students with autism will sometimes feel ganged up on or express feelings of inadequacy. It is important that the Ambassador address these feelings anytime they enter the picture.

AMBASSADOR:	That's silly; a desk is only a desk. They are all pretty much the same.
STUDENT:	Then why does he need a different desk?
AMBASSADOR:	It is more about the placement and position of the desk. We switch so that everyone can hear and see the same things. Let's try it for just a few seconds, then we can switch back.
STUDENT:	[starts to flap hands again]
AMBASSADOR:	Use your words.

> Should the student revert to flapping or any other form of nonverbal expression, the Ambassador should remind the student to use his words as many times as necessary.

STUDENT: Okay, just for a few seconds.

The student with autism stands up and the other student sits in his desk.

STUDENT: [whines]

AMBASSADOR: I know—let's count to five.

STUDENT: [counts to five]

AMBASSADOR: Good counting! Okay, now you can switch back.

> Counting is frequently used as a coping mechanism for students with autism. Ambassadors can teach students in these situations to count in order to offset their anxiety, although Ambassadors should emphasize that students need to count softly so as not to disrupt the class.

> Even though it might seem inconsequential, the Ambassador should compliment the student for successfully counting to ten, because it reinforces the positive choice the student has made in assuaging his anxiety.

The two students switch back again.

AMBASSADOR: Okay, now let's switch again.

STUDENT: [whines]

AMBASSADOR: Use your words.

STUDENT: I don't want to switch.

AMBASSADOR: Just for ten seconds this time. We have to switch so that every student gets a chance to sit in every part of the classroom, so they can hear and see the same things.

> The Ambassador needs to repeat the reason behind the switching of the desks, even though she just mentioned it a minute or two ago. She should never underestimate the level of anxiety that can come about as a result of changes in the routines of these students.

> As mentioned in other modules, counting is an excellent self-regulation exercise. Little by little, the Ambassador should try to ease the student away from having to count at all. Thus we start with a ten-count, then reduce it to a five-count, et cetera.

STUDENT: [counts to ten]

AMBASSADOR: Good job counting! Okay, now switch back.

The students switch back.

AMBASSADOR: Okay, now let's try it for the whole class this time.

STUDENT: [flaps]

AMBASSADOR: Use your words.

STUDENT: No, I don't want to switch for the whole class.

AMBASSADOR: But don't you want to be fair to (other student's name)? And you're doing such a great job sitting in that other desk. I know you're going to love sitting there once you get used to it.

STUDENT: [looks away]

AMBASSADOR: You can count to five, then to ten, okay?

STUDENT: Okay.

The students switch desks.

AMBASSADOR: Good switch! Now let's get started with our class.

STUDENT: [counts to ten, then counts to five, then is quiet]

AMBASSADOR: (Student's name), great job being calm!

Outro

The objective was to teach students with autism how to calm themselves down when desks are switched. We began by switching desks briefly, then teaching the student with autism how to regulate his response accordingly. Ambassadors should be prepared to use steps like the ones we used incrementally until the student puts up little to no resistance to the desks being switched.

As with all other modules, it is imperative that Ambassadors anticipate distracting situations that might arise and use their training to refocus the student's attention back on the task at hand. If necessary, it is fine for the Ambassador to improvise, as long as the improvisation falls well within the range of acceptable behavior. Should more assistance be necessary, the Ambassador should not hesitate to engage a teacher or parent supervisor.

Watching a Video in Class

*An Autism Ambassadors
Original Module*

Intro

The purpose of this module is to get students to sit quietly and watch a video as it's being played for a classroom, which is a typical part of a middle or high school student's daily experience.

Video watching, while a relatively unstructured activity, still requires students to be part of a group and focus their attention on something for an extended period of time. Our curriculum sections teach all of these skills; however, this module focuses specifically on teaching the student to sit quietly and pay attention to a video, which, due to a variety of factors, might provide a number of opportunities for distraction for students with autism.

This module takes place at the student's desk in school. Schools will often assign a specific desk to each student. To simulate this situation, you can use a sharpie to mark a letter or a number on a piece of paper and then tape it on the desk or chair. In our exercise, we have put a felt *A* on the desk where we want the student to sit. To replicate a classroom setting, we need other students, which we will select from among the students in Ambassador training. All Ambassador trainees role-play and take turns being the student with autism. The student simulators will sit at desks near the student with autism, while another student will sit in a teacher's chair.

As with all of our other modules, should the student show signs of extended disengagement or display self-stimulatory behavior with her hands, the Ambassador should refer to our introductory module **Pay Attention/Calm Hands** in order to get the student to be fully present for the lesson.

We are now ready to begin.

AMBASSADOR: (Student's name), today we're going to watch a video.

STUDENT: [sits down, starts playing with hands]

AMBASSADOR: Sometimes we watch videos in class that are like the movies we see in the movie theater, only in these videos the stories are not made up.

STUDENT: [starts to fidget; looks away]

AMBASSADOR: Do you have a favorite movie?

STUDENT: [nods]

AMBASSADOR: What's your favorite movie?

> It is important for the Ambassador to do whatever he can to keep the student engaged. So if the video that's being shown isn't a movie, the Ambassador should ask the student about television shows or anything else relevant to the video being shown. Ultimately the ambassador should bring the conversation back to the focus of the video being shown in class that day.

STUDENT: I like trains.

> As discussed in other modules, students with autism frequently use non sequiturs. Ambassadors should gently redirect the student back to the topic at hand.

AMBASSADOR: I like trains, too, but there aren't any in this video. What is your favorite movie (or TV show)?

STUDENT: (names a movie or TV show, or something else)

AMBASSADOR: I like that movie (or TV show), too. But today we're going to watch something different. It's a video, and it's about (subject of video).

STUDENT: [starts whining]

AMBASSADOR: You know what I like about this video? It's really similar to the movie you like.

> Given the need to improvise in this exercise, the Ambassador should be familiar with the video that's being shown and should be ready to compare it to several other titles in order to quell the anxiety of the student. Should the two titles have nothing in common—for example, if the student mentioned the Pixar movie *Cars,* whereas the class video is about the Civil War—the Ambassador should use the most general of language to compare the two. In this case, the Ambassador might suggest that they're both really interesting stories, but *Cars* is about the relationships between cars, and this Civil War video is about the relationship between the North and South that turned ugly and led to war.

The lights go out. The student appears nervous and starts flapping her hands and making clucking sounds.

AMBASSADOR: When you go to the movies, do you sometimes have a snack?

STUDENT: I like candy.

AMBASSADOR: Me, too, but we can't have candy now. Would you like a banana?

> The Ambassador should check beforehand with the teacher to ensure that snacks are permitted during video watching, but most teachers will accommodate a student with special needs, especially if introducing a familiar part of the student's movie-watching rituals (e.g., eating candy) will help quell any anxiety on the part of the student that arises from suddenly being asked to sit in a darkened room in the middle of the school day.

STUDENT: I would like a banana.

AMBASSADOR: Great. I would like a banana, too.

The Ambassador and student eat bananas.

STUDENT: I like this movie!

AMBASSADOR :   Me, too!

Outro

In this module, we started by teaching our Ambassadors about the video being shown so they could find a way to make the video feel familiar to the student. We taught the Ambassador how to anticipate any anxiety the student might feel on account of this new ritual and how to introduce something from that student's movie-watching ritual into the experience to address this anxiety.

As we mentioned in the learning moments, this will not come easily to the assigned students, nor will it come easily to the Ambassadors. However, over the course of time and with increased experience watching videos, the skills to keep themselves occupied will be presented enough times so that students with autism can pay attention and not be disruptive to other students who are trying to watch. As with all other modules, it is imperative that Ambassadors anticipate distracting situations that might arise and use their training to refocus the student's attention back on the task at hand. If necessary, it is fine for the Ambassador to improvise, as long as the improvisation falls well within the range of acceptable behavior. Should more assistance be necessary, the Ambassador should not hesitate to ask the teacher.

Writing an Intro Paragraph

*An Autism Ambassadors
Original Module*

Intro

The purpose of this lesson is to teach students with autism how to write an introductory paragraph along the lines of the cone structure taught in most contemporary high school English classrooms. Students with autism frequently struggle with organizational skills (see our module **Organizing Notebooks** for more on this topic), but they love structure, because it provides order to a world that, to them, frequently seems disjointed and disorienting. Teaching students to write an intro paragraph, using a rigid structural rubric, not only helps them with their academic endeavors, it allows them to see that there are other opportunities to apply their sense of order in the world.

This module takes place at the student's desk in school. Schools will often assign a specific desk to each student. To simulate this situation, you can use a sharpie to mark a letter or a number on a piece of paper and then tape it on the desk or chair. In our exercise, we have put a felt *A* on the desk where we want the student to sit. To replicate a classroom setting, we need other students, which we will select from among the students in Ambassador training. All Ambassador trainees role-play and take turns being the student who needs assistance.

In your modeling of this situation, if a different student has taken the seat assigned to the student with autism, prompt the student with autism to politely ask the typical student to move.

The Ambassador should also have a sno-cone as a demonstration tool for this exercise. If no sno-cone is available, the Ambassador should use a cone-shaped piece of paper mache that's colored like a sno-cone. The Ambassador should also have a whiteboard and marker to pass back and forth with the student; please refer to our module **Passing the Baton** for additional tips on this subject.

As with all of our other modules, should the student show signs of extended disengagement or display self-stimulatory behavior with his hands, the Ambassador should refer to our introductory module **Pay Attention/Calm Hands** in order to get the student to be fully present for the lesson.

We are now ready to begin. The Ambassador and the student with autism are sitting at their desks.

AMBASSADOR:	(Student's name), today we are going to write an introductory paragraph to an essay.
STUDENT:	[looks away, uninterested]
AMBASSADOR:	An introductory paragraph is important because it sets up what you're going to be writing about.
STUDENT:	How?
AMBASSADOR:	It's like setting the table for a fancy meal. If you were going to eat a nice meal, how would you set the table?
STUDENT:	With a nice tablecloth, and fancy china, and beautiful silverware, and matching napkins and a centerpiece and maybe some fancy decorative fruit....

Even if the student rambles on, as this student is doing, the Ambassador should allow him to do so. The learning moment involves making an analogy that the student understands comprehensively, thus enabling him to understand how to apply the underlying principles to the exercise at hand.

AMBASSADOR:	Right. So if we're going to be writing an essay, our introductory paragraph is going to set the table for the rest of what we're going to be writing about. Think of all the pieces we're about to discuss as pieces that go on the table to set up a nice meal, okay?
STUDENT:	Okay.
AMBASSADOR:	First let's discuss what we're going to be writing about. Do you have an essay due in any class?
STUDENT:	I have an essay due on *The Catcher in the Rye* for English class.
AMBASSADOR:	Okay. We're going to think of our intro paragraph like a sno-cone.
STUDENT:	Can we eat it?

The cone structure is very much in accordance with the way writing is taught in most schools today. It teaches that the introductory paragraph begins with more general tidbits of information, which are followed by more and more specific pieces of information, until the writer reaches the thesis statement and topic sentence.

> The student answers with a bit of whimsy; Ambassadors should be ready to engage the whimsy and, if at all possible, work it into the exercise.

AMBASSADOR: Ha, no; just like we are comparing food on a table to words in a paragraph, the cone is a comparison. We're going to be shaping our thoughts like a cone. [pulls out the sno-cone (or paper mache cone)] We are going to start with a big, general thought, and then get more and more specific.

STUDENT: I don't understand.

AMBASSADOR: Here, let's use the cone: You know how when you lick the top of the cone, there's less flavor, but the closer you get to the bottom of the cone, the more flavorful it is? [ambassador demonstrates with the cone] That's the same way general and specific thoughts work. We're going to start with a category that's really big and includes a lot of smaller categories, and then work our way down to the end of the paragraph and get into more specific categories, until we have no more specific categories.

STUDENT: Show me.

AMBASSADOR: Okay. Let's say I was writing an essay about Kobe Bryant, the star basketball player for the Lakers. First I might write something about basketball, because that is the biggest, most general category. Then I might write something about the Lakers, because that is more specific and is part of the basketball category. Then I might write something about Kobe Bryant, because that is the most specific part and is part of both the Lakers and the basketball categories.

> In addition to the physical cone, the Ambassador should feel free to use a whiteboard and marker to demonstrate the evolution of the paragraph from more general to more specific. The Ambassador should write down the words *basketball, Lakers,* and *Kobe Bryant* and place them atop each other in the proper order.

AMBASSADOR: So my first thought might be that basketball has had many great scorers in its history. My second thought might be that the Lakers have had many of them and have won many championships as a result. And my final thought might be that Kobe Bryant is one of the greatest Lakers and basketball players of all time.

The Ambassador now hands the cone and whiteboard pen over to the student.

AMBASSADOR: Okay, your turn: What do you want to say about *The Catcher in the Rye?*

STUDENT: It's a book about sports.

> The student might try to find an association related to what the Ambassador just discussed (in this case, sports) or might just veer off course for a variety of reasons. The Ambassador needs to steer the student back on track without being off-putting.

AMBASSADOR: You know what, I know it sounds like a book about sports, and the main character probably enjoys sports. But I don't think that's what *The Catcher in the Rye* is about. First, let's think about a more general category. Remember how I first talked about basketball? What's the most general category you can use here?

STUDENT: Books?

AMBASSADOR: Good thinking! So let's put that at the top of the cone.

STUDENT: [writes the word *books* on the whiteboard]

AMBASSADOR: What comes in the more specific category?

STUDENT: The book's title.

AMBASSADOR: Great! And then after that?

STUDENT: Holden Caulfield.

AMBASSADOR: Fantastic! So let's write all that down.

> If the student cannot come to these conclusions on his own, the Ambassador should write down three ideas—one general, one more specific, one completely specific—on the board, and have the student order them from the most general to the most specific. They should practice this several times, until the student can order the words confidently.

AMBASSADOR: Okay, now let's try to figure out what you want to say about these three categories.

STUDENT: I have read many books, but I like *The Catcher in the Rye* the best. And Holden Caulfield is my favorite character of all time.

AMBASSADOR: Great job! Now let's go back to my cone. [takes the marker and starts writing on the whiteboard] The reasons why I think Kobe Bryant is one of the greatest basketball players of all time is because he has won five championships, several scoring titles, and one MVP award.

The Ambassador hands the marker back to the student.

AMBASSADOR: What are some of the reasons why Holden Caulfield is your favorite character of all time?

STUDENT: Because he likes sports.

AMBASSADOR: That might be true, but let's try to think about what was in the book that made you like him so much.

STUDENT: Because he was really nice to his sister, he didn't like pho-
               nies at all, and he knew how to walk all around New York
               City without any help from a grown-up.

AMBASSADOR: Great reasons! Write them down on the whiteboard; then let's
               go write your intro paragraph!

Outro

Using the cone structure and some visual aids, the Ambassador identified and taught the student how to identify the more general categories of
a topic, and then whittled them down to more and more specific subtopics
to arrive at a thesis statement. The Ambassador used this as a springboard
to identify three body paragraph topic sentences, which we will learn
about in a module later in the book. Following successful implementation
of this exercise, the Ambassador should then sit with the student and write
the actual paragraph, making a point of writing her own alongside the
student.

As with all other modules, it is imperative that Ambassadors anticipate
distracting situations that might arise and use their training to refocus the
student's attention back on the task at hand. If necessary, it is fine for the
Ambassador to improvise, as long as the improvisation falls well within
the range of acceptable behavior. Should more assistance be necessary, the
Ambassador should not hesitate to ask the teacher.

Writing a
Chunk Paragraph

*An Autism Ambassadors
Original Module*

Intro

The purpose of this module is to teach students with autism how to write a chunk paragraph along the lines of the chunk body paragraph structure taught in most high school English classrooms. Students with autism frequently struggle with organizational skills (see our module **Organizing Notebooks** for more on this topic), but they love structure, because it provides order to a world that, to them, frequently seems disjointed and disorienting. Teaching students to write chunk paragraphs, using a rigid structural rubric, not only helps them with their academic endeavors, it allows them to see that there are other opportunities to apply their sense of order in the world.

This module takes place at the student's desk in school. Schools will often assign a specific desk to each student. To simulate this situation, you can use a sharpie to mark a letter or a number on a piece of paper and then tape it on the desk or chair. In our exercise, we have put a felt *A* on the desk where we want the student to sit. To replicate a classroom setting, we need other students, which we will select from among the students in Ambassador training. All Ambassador trainees role-play and take turns being the student who needs assistance. In your modeling of this situation, if a different student has taken the seat assigned to the student with autism, prompt the student with autism to politely ask the typical student to move.

The Ambassador should also have a brownie with chocolate chips available; this will come in handy for demonstrations and will serve as a handy incentive to boot. (Note: Should the student with autism be allergic to such treats, as many students with autism are, the Ambassador should substitute either a gluten/casein-free brownie, or a chunk of Play-Doh with different colored pieces in it.) The Ambassador should also have a whiteboard and marker to pass back and forth with the student; please refer to our module **Passing the Baton** for additional tips on this subject.

This module should be done in conjunction with our **Writing an Intro Paragraph** module, and the chunk body paragraph assembled in this module should be a continuation of the intro paragraph established in that module.

As with all of our other modules, should the student show signs of extended disengagement or display self-stimulatory behavior with his hands, the Ambassador should refer to our introductory module **Pay Attention/Calm Hands** in order to get the student to be fully present for the lesson.

We are now ready to begin. The Ambassador and the student with autism are sitting at their desks.

AMBASSADOR: (Student's name), today we are going to write a chunk paragraph as part of the essay we began the other day.

STUDENT: [looks away, uninterested]

AMBASSADOR: Body paragraphs are important because they give our essay the supporting information it needs to feel fully fleshed out.

STUDENT: Why?

AMBASSADOR: Remember what we said when we talked about our intro paragraph, about how it was like setting the table for a fancy meal? Our chunk paragraphs are the fancy meal.

> The Ambassador is extending the metaphor that she began in the other module, **Writing an Intro Paragraph,** further; these exercises should be done in tandem, with many of the same principles and examples cross-referenced.

STUDENT: Okay.

AMBASSADOR: Remember how we used the cone for the intro paragraphs? Today we are going to use a brownie to demonstrate our chunk paragraphs.

STUDENT: Can we eat the brownie?

> Even though the student should, in all likelihood, be able to infer from the way the sno-cone was used in the **Writing an Intro Paragraph** module that the brownie is not for eating, it is distinctly possible that he might still wish to look past the figurative part of the exercise. Ambassadors should be ready to engage the student's desire to eat the brownie and, if at all possible, work it into the exercise. Should the Ambassador be using Play-Doh, she should substitute the words *play with* for the word *eat*, and proceed accordingly.

AMBASSADOR: Ha, no; just like earlier, when we were comparing food on a table to words in a paragraph, the brownie is a comparison. We're going to be building our body paragraph the way a brownie is made. [pulls out the brownie (or Play-Doh)] Each paragraph is made up of two big ideas. These are called chunks. Inside those ideas are details that make that idea true. Those are called supporting details.

STUDENT: I don't understand.

AMBASSADOR: Here, let's use the brownie to demonstrate: See how the brownie is mostly made up of chocolate cake? But it's got these chocolate chips inside of it? Think of the brownie as the chunk, the cake as the idea, and the chips as the supporting details.

> Should the student be unable to follow the example as outlined above, the Ambassador should break it down into individual steps and use the whiteboard as a supplementary teaching tool, drawing visual comparisons between the brownie (or Play-Doh) and the chunk approach to writing.

AMBASSADOR: That's the same way ideas and supporting details work. We're going to start with a big idea and then come up with two supporting details for that big idea.

STUDENT: Show me.

AMBASSADOR: Okay. Remember my essay about Kobe Bryant, the star basketball player for the Lakers? My first point about why he was my favorite basketball player was that he was the most important reason the Lakers won five championships. So that's my chunk.

> The Ambassador should feel free to use the whiteboard and marker throughout this example to demonstrate the evolution of the paragraph from big idea through supporting details.

AMBASSADOR: Now my supporting details are as follows: The Lakers had other great players, but Kobe Bryant was their leading scorer; during the championship series, he averaged nearly 30 points per game. That's my first supporting detail. My second supporting detail is that every time the Lakers needed someone to make an important basket when the game was close to being lost, Kobe Bryant was able to do that for them. That's my second supporting detail.

The Ambassador now hands the brownie and whiteboard pen over to the student.

AMBASSADOR: Okay, your turn: remember what you said about *The Catcher in the Rye?*

STUDENT: It's a book about delicious food.

> The student might try to find an association related to what he is looking at, or he might just veer off course for a variety of reasons. The Ambassador needs to steer the student back on track without being off-putting.

AMBASSADOR: You know what, I know it sounds like a book about delicious food, and the main character probably enjoys delicious food. But I don't think that's what you said. Remember what you said about Holden Caulfield?

STUDENT: He is my favorite character in the history of books.

AMBASSADOR: Great job! And do you remember the reasons why?

STUDENT: Because he was really nice to his sister, he didn't like phonies at all, and he knew how to walk all around New York City without any help from a grown-up.

AMBASSADOR: Which one of those do you want to be your first chunk?

> If the student cannot make a decision, the Ambassador should attempt to figure out which point the student seems to feel he is most partial to. As the Ambassador does this, the student's thinking process might open up, which will help him list and explore the supporting details.

STUDENT: I like the part where he was nice to his sister.

AMBASSADOR: Great! Me, too. Can you give me two examples where he was nice to his sister?

> Refer to our module **Finding Favorite Books,** especially the latter part of the module, in which we teach students how to do research.

STUDENT: He went to go pick her up at her school, and he took her ice skating.

AMBASSADOR: Great exploring! Now let's explore a little bit deeper. I'm going to go back to my brownie. [takes the marker to write on the whiteboard] I want a conclusion to my paragraph.

STUDENT: Why?

AMBASSADOR: Because otherwise it just sits there without an ending. It would be like someone chopped the ending off your favorite movie and then expected you to like it as much.

> It is important for the Ambassador to explain herself not only in detail, but by using as many relevant analogies as possible, giving the student ample opportunity to understand why these aspects of the exercise are important.

AMBASSADOR: I'm going to conclude that because Kobe Bryant averaged nearly 30 points a game in the championships, and because he always gave the Lakers an important basket when they needed it, that he is not just a great player, but a truly special player, a once-in-a-lifetime player.

The Ambassador hands the marker over to the student.

AMBASSADOR: Now what can you conclude about Holden Caulfield?

STUDENT: I'm going to conclude that because he was nice to his sister, he was not the jerk he thinks he wants to be. He is really a nice guy.

AMBASSADOR: Great conclusion! I agree with you!

Outro

Using the chunk structure and some visual aids, the Ambassador taught how to identify topic sentence ideas and then further develop them using supporting details. Once this had been achieved, the Ambassador taught the student how to use those details to lead to a resolution of the topic sentence. Following successful implementation of this exercise, the Ambassador should then sit with the student and write the actual paragraph, making a point of writing her own alongside the student.

As with all other modules, it is imperative that Ambassadors anticipate distracting situations that might arise and use their training to refocus the student's attention back on the task at hand. If necessary, it is fine for the Ambassador to improvise, as long as the improvisation falls well within the range of acceptable behavior. Should more assistance be necessary, the Ambassador should not hesitate to ask the teacher.

Writing a Concluding Paragraph

An Autism Ambassadors Original Module

Intro

The purpose of this module is to teach students with autism how to write a concluding paragraph along the lines of the pyramid structure taught in most contemporary high school English classrooms. Students with autism frequently have terrible organizational skills (see our module **Organizing Notebooks** for more on this topic), but they love structure, because it provides order to a world that, to them, frequently seems disjointed and disorienting. Teaching students to write a concluding paragraph, using a rigid structural rubric, not only helps them with their academic endeavors, it allows them to see that there are other opportunities to apply their sense of order in the world.

This module takes place at the student's desk in school. Schools will often assign a specific desk to each student. To simulate this situation, you can use a sharpie to mark a letter or a number on a piece of paper and then tape it on the desk or chair. In our exercise, we have put a felt *A* on the desk where we want the student to sit. To replicate a classroom setting, we need other students, which we will select from among the students in Ambassador training. All Ambassador trainees role-play and take turns being the student who needs assistance. In your modeling of this situation, if a different student has taken the seat assigned to the student with autism, prompt the student with autism to politely ask the typical student to move.

The Ambassador should have either a simulated Egyptian-style pyramid (the kind classrooms use to study ancient Egypt) or a self-made pyramid that can be fashioned out of paper mache. The Ambassador should also have a whiteboard and marker to share with the student; please refer to our module **Passing the Baton** for additional tips on this subject.

This module should be done in conjunction with, and following, our modules **Writing an Intro Paragraph** and **Writing a Chunk Paragraph**.

As with all of our other modules, should the student show signs of extended disengagement or display self-stimulatory behavior with his hands, the Ambassador should refer to our introductory module **Pay Attention/Calm Hands** in order to get the student to be fully present for the lesson.

We are now ready to begin. The Ambassador and the student with autism are sitting at their desks.

AMBASSADOR: (Student's name), today we are going to write a concluding paragraph to the essay we began.

STUDENT: [looks away, uninterested]

AMBASSADOR: A concluding paragraph is important because it allows us to finish our story.

STUDENT: So?

AMBASSADOR: So remember how when we were writing our chunk paragraph, we found a way to conclude it? Remember how we finished our story so that everyone was satisfied?

STUDENT: Oh yeah. It would be like if at the end of *Titanic*, the boat didn't sink but instead Leonardo DiCaprio and Kate Winslet kept sailing on the boat, and Kate Winslet's fiancée was still angry with her because she wanted to be with Leonardo DiCaprio.

> Even if the student rambles on, as this student is doing, the Ambassador should allow him to do so. The learning moment involves making an analogy that the student understands comprehensively, thus enabling him to understand how to apply the underlying principles to the exercise at hand.

AMBASSADOR: Right. So if we're going to be writing an essay, our concluding paragraph is going to be like an ending to a great movie. It will make the reader enjoy it much more, just like you enjoyed the ending of *Titanic*, okay?

STUDENT: Okay.

AMBASSADOR: Okay. We're going to think of our concluding paragraph like a pyramid.

STUDENT: Like in Egypt? Can we climb it?

> The pyramid structure is very much in accordance with the way writing is taught in most schools today. It teaches that the concluding paragraph begins with more specific tidbits of information, which are followed by more and more general pieces of information until the writer reaches the concluding statement.

> The student answers with a bit of whimsy; Ambassadors should be ready to engage the whimsy and, if at all possible, work it into the exercise.

AMBASSADOR: Ha, no. But you can think of it like climbing if you like. [pulls out the pyramid] Remember how we wrote our intro paragraph? How we started with a big, general thought, and then got more and more specific? This time we're going to do the exact opposite.

> The Ambassador should refer to what she wrote down during the **Writing the Intro Paragraph** module and show how she can flip it around to fulfill the needs of the concluding paragraph.

STUDENT: Why?

AMBASSADOR: Because we just spent the last three paragraphs being really specific, even though we began the essay with a general idea. Now we want to branch back out to something general so we leave the readers feeling the same way they did when they began reading.

> The Ambassador needs to emphasize the inverse effect—that the end of an essay has to perform the same function as the end of a movie. Should the Ambassador wish, she can liken this structure to that of most Hollywood movies: The audience enters happy, starts off with happy characters, and then watches them go through something that challenges them, but in the end they go back to being happy.

STUDENT: Okay.

AMBASSADOR: Okay. So remember my essay about Kobe Bryant? How I talked all about how he was one of the greatest basketball players of all time? Now I'm going to start my concluding paragraph at the top of the pyramid with something specific and sharp and pointy.

> In addition to the pyramid, the Ambassador should feel free to use a whiteboard and marker to demonstrate the evolution of the paragraph from more general to more specific.

AMBASSADOR: So my first concluding thought is going to repeat that Kobe Bryant is one of the greatest basketball players of all time.

The Ambassador now hands the pyramid, whiteboard, and marker over to the student.

AMBASSADOR: Okay, your turn: what's your first concluding thought going to be?

STUDENT: That I was sorry when the Titanic sank.

> The student might try to find an association related to what the Ambassador discussed earlier (the movie *Titanic*) or might just veer off course for a variety of reasons. The Ambassador needs to steer the student back on track without being off-putting.

AMBASSADOR: You know what, I was sorry when the Titanic sank, too. But remember, your essay is about *The Catcher in the Rye* and how Holden Caulfield was one of your favorite book characters of all time. So let's try to come up with something really specific about Holden Caulfield.

STUDENT: Okay. I like how nice Holden Caulfield was to his sister and how cool a guy he seemed to be.

AMBASSADOR: Good thinking! So let's put that at the top of the pyramid.

The student writes down his thoughts about Holden Caulfield on the whiteboard and hands the pen and whiteboard back to the Ambassador.

AMBASSADOR: Okay, now I'm going to write down something a little more general about Kobe Bryant. I'm going to say that Kobe Bryant is the symbol of everything the Lakers stand for.

The Ambassador writes this down, and then passes the marker and whiteboard to the student.

STUDENT: Now I'm going to write down something a little more general. I'm going to say that Holden Caulfield is the symbol of all the things that make teenagers sad.

> Going from specific points to general points is a hard lesson to learn even for typical students; for students with autism, who struggle with simple issues of relevance and linear progression in conversation, let alone in essays, it is nearly impossible without impeccable guidance. Thus, it is the job of the Ambassador to draw clean logic lines, from specific to general, that are easy for the student to emulate, as exemplified above.

The Ambassador takes the marker and whiteboard from the student.

AMBASSADOR: Great point! Lastly, for my most general point, I'm going to say that Kobe Bryant's accomplishments as a player and champion should make him a candidate for the basketball Hall of Fame.

The Ambassador hands the marker and whiteboard over to the student.

STUDENT: For my most general point, I'm going to say that Holden Caulfield is the kind of kid that everyone should be as a friend.

AMBASSADOR: Great reasons! Write them down on the whiteboard, and then let's go write your concluding paragraph!

Outro

Using the pyramid structure and some visual aids, the Ambassador taught the student to identify the more specific categories of a topic and then to develop the points into more general points until a conclusion was drawn. The Ambassador drew upon the lessons learned, and essays begun, in our earlier modules, **Writing an Intro Paragraph** and **Writing a Chunk Paragraph.**

As with the related modules, following successful implementation of this exercise, the Ambassador should sit with the student and write the actual paragraph, making a point of writing her own alongside the student. As with all other modules, it is imperative that Ambassadors anticipate distracting situations that might arise and use their training to refocus the student's attention back on the task at hand. If necessary, it is fine for the Ambassador to improvise, as long as the improvisation falls well within the range of acceptable behavior. Should more assistance be necessary, the Ambassador should not hesitate to ask the teacher.

School-Related/ Out-of-Class Modules

S chools are facing massive reductions in their already-thin resources due to budget cuts, and nowhere is this more evident than in the special education departments of virtually every school in America. When students with autism act out and disrupt their environments, they put more responsibility on the shoulders of their teachers to cater to them. We feel it is the job of the Ambassador to help students with autism integrate themselves into the school environment, assisting in the classroom and helping teachers in this endeavor. Ambassadors can achieve these goals with the help of the modules in this section, all of which take place on school grounds and pertain to the academic environment but are not themselves academic in nature.

The six lesson plans that make up this section are as follows:

1. Fire/Emergency Drill

2. Getting to Class on Time

3. Organizing Your Time

4. Finding Favorite Books

5. Organizing Notebooks

6. Study Hall

The **Fire/Emergency Drill** module teaches what may be the important lesson students with autism need to learn, for obvious reasons. In addition to natural disasters, which are a perennial threat for schools (more in some regions than others), recent years have seen a disturbing rise in school shootings. Principals and school administrators have made great strides in creating contingency plans for these tragic events, but they are only as effective as the ability of the students participating in them to remain calm and follow protocol. This module desensitizes students with autism to noise and teaches them how to redirect their feelings of anxiety.

Getting to Class on Time provides a handy tool for students who find themselves distracted from time to time (and what school-aged student doesn't find herself in this predicament on a near-daily basis in this era of handheld electronic devices?), but it is especially useful for students with autism because it addresses the significant time management issues students with autism face when navigating the hallways en route from one class to another. This is especially true when those students have to stop at their lockers, or get approached by friends, or face one of a whole host of distractions that transpire between any given point A to any given point B. This lesson plan teaches these easily distracted students how to stay on task, so they do not disrupt their classrooms with chronic tardiness.

Organizing Notebooks teaches basic organization principles to students with autism whose disorganization issues tend to range beyond those that are characteristic of teenagers. Many students with autism do not make associative connections between school subject materials and anything else they have been given in their classes, and thus these materials wind up dumped carelessly in their backpacks and notebooks without any consideration for where they should logically be placed. The principles covered in this module can be carried over to modules like **Organizing Your Time** and **Getting to Class on Time,** and help students organize themselves so that tests and homework are simply a cognitive issue, not an operational one as well.

Organizing Your Time can be taught in tandem with **Getting to Class on Time** because both modules pertain to the academic arena but involve teaching essential life skills that students can apply outside school. Although this module pertains to students' ability to finish their homework at home, it can also be taught in association with **Making a Plan,** which helps students with autism organize their social lives and can be found in the Social Skills section of this book.

Finding Favorite Books is a two-part module that first teaches students with autism how to find books in the school library that they may wish to read. The module then shifts to address how students can first identify and then find books they might need for school-related research projects. This is a library-based module, so students and Ambassadors will need permission and assistance from the school librarian prior to moving forward. Ambassadors also need to be aware of any issues with sensory input or noise volume that might pertain to their students and must factor these into working in a library.

Study Hall draws upon principles first addressed in our modules **Being Alone** and **Organizing Your Time** to teach students with autism how to function in a school's all-important study hall period. If students can finish much of their homework during study hall, they will face less pressure during their time after school. This will in turn have a positive effect on their anxiety and allow them to explore and apply the principles they learned in our **Making a Plan** and **Organizing Your Time** modules.

Fire/Emergency Drill

An Autism Ambassadors
Original Module

Intro

The purpose of this module is to help students with autism react appropriately to an emergency drill in school, whether it be for a fire, flood, tornado, or earthquake. Students with autism, in addition to having tactile and anxiety-related issues, frequently experience difficulty when they are exposed to loud noises. Under most school-related circumstances, this poses no problem. However, fire and emergency drills are typically announced with a loud siren, which can potentially provoke the student with autism into acting in a way that can undermine the steps students and faculty must take for these drills to be successful.

This module takes place first in a playground area (for the desensitization part of the exercise) and then at the student's desk in school, where we will enact the actual drill. Schools will often assign a specific desk to each student. To simulate this situation, you can use a sharpie to mark a letter or a number on a piece of paper and then tape it on the desk or chair. In our exercise, we have put a felt *A* on the desk where we want the student to sit. To replicate a classroom setting, we need other students, which we will select from among the students in Ambassador training. All Ambassador trainees role-play and take turns being the student with autism. The student simulators will sit at desks near the student with autism while another student will sit in a teacher's chair. The Ambassador should be seated right next to the student with autism. We will also need a bullhorn, or any similar instrument capable of creating a loud noise to simulate the drill. As with all of our other modules, should the student show signs of extended disengagement or display self-stimulatory behavior with her hands, the Ambassador should refer to our introductory module **Pay Attention/Calm Hands** in order to get the student to be fully present for the lesson.

We are now ready to begin. The student and Ambassador walk onto the playground.

AMBASSADOR: (Student's name), do you want to play a game?

STUDENT: Yes.

AMBASSADOR: Great! Me, too! Let's play a game with this bullhorn: I'll hit the noise maker, and when I do, you get to go running anywhere you want until it stops. Does that sound like fun?

STUDENT: [nods head]

> Should the student be unreceptive to this, the Ambassador should allow the student to be the one to press the bullhorn button first, and the Ambassador should be the one to run. Then the two can switch places and the exercise can proceed as follows. The Ambassador should also feel free to substitute anything that he feels might be more amenable to the student, based on the preferences of that student (e.g., collecting dandelions, pointing out airplanes, etc.).

AMBASSADOR: Great. Ready? Set? Go!

The Ambassador hits the noise maker, and the student starts to run around the playground.

> The Ambassador is desensitizing the student to the loud noise by first associating it with something fun (i.e., running around on the playground). Should the student have an adverse reaction to the noise, the Ambassador should stop immediately and desensitize the student by allowing the student to be the one making the noise, as outlined above.

AMBASSADOR: Great playing! Now let's try a different game: I'm going to make the noise, but instead of running around, we're going to walk silently in a line together over to the door.

STUDENT: [looks nervous]

AMBASSADOR: I've got a great idea: You can be the leader. Would you like that?

STUDENT: Okay.

> The Ambassador should employ any tactics he can to incentivize the student. Should the above technique not work, the Ambassador should feel free to incorporate different incentives or objectives, such as collecting items, getting cookies or a snack in the lunch area, et cetera. Since the emergency drill will always require an end objective (exiting the room), the Ambassador should always try to work one into the situation at hand.

AMBASSADOR: Great! Remember, it's important to be completely quiet during this game. Ready? Set? Go!

The Ambassador and student walk in a silent line together over to the door that leads from the playground to the cafeteria.

AMBASSADOR: Great game! Now let's play that game with a bunch of other students!

> Refer to our sports modules—**Playing Soccer, Playing Football,** et cetera—for additional tips on how to integrate students with autism into playground games.

The Ambassador leads the student over to a group of other Ambassadors and presses the bullhorn noisemaker. The Ambassadors line up and walk over to the door along with the student with autism.

The student with autism enters the classroom and sits down at her desk. The Ambassador sits down at a desk next to the student with autism.

AMBASSADOR: This time, we are going to do the same thing we did outside, only we're going to do it inside.

STUDENT: But I like playing outside better.

AMBASSADOR: I do, too. But right now, we're going to practice an emergency drill. That means that we're going to practice how to exit the classroom in a quiet line, in case there's a fire or earthquake. And then we'll be outside.

> Some students with autism have considerable anxiety about disaster-related subjects. Ambassadors should use their discretion, given their knowledge of their student partners, and decide whether or not to mention the fact that the exercise is emergency related.

STUDENT: Okay.

AMBASSADOR: Great! Okay, just like last time, wait for the noise....

The Ambassador presses the bullhorn noisemaker. The other Ambassadors and the student with autism stand up and form a line, then exit outside, and then return to the classroom.

AMBASSADOR: Great game! Now we're going to play one last time, only this time I'm not going to tell you when the noise is going to happen; you're going to have to wait and then start the game on your own when you do hear it. Okay?

STUDENT: Okay.

The Ambassadors and student take their seats. One of the Ambassadors purposely sets off his cell phone. The student with autism stands up.

AMBASSADOR: (Student's name), great playing, but we only play when we hear the loud alarm sound, not just any sound, okay?

STUDENT: Okay.

> In order not to isolate the student with autism, it is probably a good idea for several other Ambassadors to rise as well when they hear the cell phone go off; this way the student with autism will not feel foolish.

The Ambassador waits for a bit, and then presses the bullhorn noisemaker. All the Ambassadors, as well as the student with autism, stand up and exit in a single file line.

AMBASSADOR: Great playing!

Outro

The goal of the module was to teach students with autism how to exit the classroom during an emergency drill. Because these students frequently have adverse reactions to sudden, loud noises, we presented the exercise in stages that allowed the student to become desensitized to the alarm. Eventually, the student was able to react appropriately to the sound of the alarm and participate in the drill in spontaneous fashion.

As with all other modules, it is imperative that Ambassadors anticipate distracting situations that might arise and use their training to refocus the student's attention back on the task at hand. If necessary, it is fine for the Ambassador to improvise, as long as the improvisation falls well within the range of acceptable behavior. Should more assistance be necessary, the Ambassador should not hesitate to engage a teacher or schoolyard supervisor.

Getting to Class on Time

An Autism Ambassadors Original Module

Intro

This module instructs Ambassadors how to teach students with autism the twists and turns of the school hallways, helping them get from point A to point B in a timely fashion while still being able to stop at their lockers and maybe even briefly chat with a friend. School hallways can be deceptively complex places; what appears to a typical student to be a simple group of passageways is, in fact, a hierarchal and logistical nightmare for students with autism, filled with students milling about and horsing around. And when students with autism must stop at their lockers to replace textbooks, drop off notebooks, and gather new ones, this environment can sometimes exacerbate their already considerable anxiety. The goal of this exercise is to desensitize students with autism to the many distractions and noises they will be facing during a typical walk through the school hallway and to help them remain focused on the task at hand.

This exercise will take place in the hallways at school during a time when students are not around (e.g., after school or on a weekend). We will require other Ambassadors to role-play everything from the student with autism to the other students in the hallways, who will be doing everything from typical student horseplay to hanging up banners and posters. We will also need another student to stand off to the side somewhat with a loud bell that she will ring in order to simulate the school bell.

As with all of our other modules, should the student show signs of extended disengagement or display self-stimulatory behavior with his hands, the Ambassador should refer to our introductory module, **Pay Attention/Calm Hands,** in order to get the student to be fully present for the lesson.

We are now ready to begin. The Ambassador and the student with autism enter the hallway and look around.

AMBASSADOR: (Student's name), today we're going to work on getting to class on time. We're going to start by walking through the hallway.

STUDENT: I already know how to walk through the hallway.

AMBASSADOR: I know you do. So let's take a walk from one class to another. I know that on Tuesdays, you have English second period, and then math third period. So let's walk from English to math. Remember, we want to make sure we get to math before the class bell rings.

The Ambassador and student walk from the English classroom to the math classroom.

AMBASSADOR: Here we are!

The Ambassador with the bell rings it loudly.

AMBASSADOR: Listen to that! You got here just in time for the bell!

Even though the student has just completed a mundane task, the Ambassador should still compliment him in an upbeat, positive tone. Additionally, should the student experience any anxiety or noise sensitivity due to the bell, please refer to our module **Fire/Emergency Drill** for tips on how to address this.

AMBASSADOR: Okay, let's do that again. But isn't there something you usually do on the way from English to math?

STUDENT: Tie my shoes?

As outlined in other modules, students with autism frequently have a hard time understanding basic relevancy. Ambassadors should always be ready for a somewhat off-topic answer and should redirect the student back to the subject at hand.

AMBASSADOR: Well, yes, you can definitely tie your shoes on the way from English to math. But what happens if you get to math class and still have your English books?

STUDENT: I'll need to get my math books.

AMBASSADOR: Right! And where will you get your math books?

STUDENT: At my locker.

AMBASSADOR: Right. So when do you want to stop at your locker?

STUDENT: After I get to math class?

Students with autism frequently struggle with putting events in the proper sequence. It is important that the Ambassador explain step-processes in these instances the same way she would a story: with a logical beginning, middle, and end. Please see our module **Linear Sequencing** for further assistance on this subject.

AMBASSADOR: It might be too late to go to your locker if you are already at math class. The bell will ring and class will begin. So after you leave English class, what are you going to want to do?

STUDENT: Go to my locker, and then go to math class.

AMBASSADOR: Great! So let's do that.

The student and the Ambassador return to the English classroom and repeat the exercise, stopping at the student's locker before going to math class. The Ambassador with the bell rings the bell.

AMBASSADOR: Great job! You made it before the bell again! Okay, let's say it's a really busy day. Lots of students are in the hallways. Let's try to do the same thing we just did with all of them around us.

The other Ambassadors enter the hallway, and the student and Ambassador make their way from the English classroom to the student's locker, and then head over to the math classroom. The bell rings.

AMBASSADOR: Great job! Let's try it again!

The other Ambassadors once again enter the hallway, and the student and Ambassador make their way from the English classroom to the student's locker, and then head over to the math classroom. This time, however, they are blocked by two students who are putting up a poster.

POSTER STUDENTS: Hi there, guys! Do you want to check out the new pep rally posters we're putting up?

STUDENT: Sure.

As the Poster Students show off their new posters, the bell rings.

AMBASSADOR: Uh oh, did you hear that? The bell rang and we're late for class. What do you think we should do next time so that doesn't happen?

STUDENT: We should walk faster?

AMBASSADOR: That might help a little bit, but I don't think that was why we were late. What did we do differently this time that we didn't do last time?

STUDENT: We talked to those kids putting up the poster.

AMBASSADOR: Right. So what do you think we should do this time?

STUDENT: We shouldn't talk to those kids putting up the poster.

AMBASSADOR: Great answer! Come on, let's try it again.

The other Ambassadors once again enter the hallway, and the student and Ambassador make their way from the English classroom to the student's locker, and then head over to the math classroom. This time, however, another Ambassador approaches the student and Ambassador before they reach the classroom.

OTHER   Hey guys. Want to see my new iPad?
AMBASSADOR:

STUDENT: Yeah. What apps do you have?

As the Other Ambassador shows the apps to the student, the bell rings again.

AMBASSADOR: Uh oh, the bell rang again. We're late.

STUDENT: But I really want to see those apps.

AMBASSADOR: I know. So I have an idea: this time, instead of stopping to talk, what can you do?

STUDENT: Walk faster?

AMBASSADOR: You can walk a little faster, but I don't think that's why you were late. If you are walking to class, and your friend with the iPad is walking to class, what can you both do so you're both not late?

STUDENT: We can both walk to class together.

> The Ambassador should always try to let the student arrive at this conclusion by himself. Problem solving is one of the most important skills an Ambassador can work on with a student with autism.

AMBASSADOR: Great answer! Let's try it again!

The other Ambassadors once again enter the hallway, and the student and Ambassador make their way from the English classroom to the student's locker, and then head over to the math classroom. This time, however, another Ambassador approaches the student and Ambassador before they reach the classroom.

OTHER   Hey guys. Want to see my new iPad?
AMBASSADOR:

STUDENT: Yeah, but I don't want to be late for class. So can we walk to class together and you can show me on the way there?

OTHER   Sure, that would be great. Come on, let's go to class!
AMBASSADOR:

Outro

The Ambassador walked the student with autism through a series of steps that grew increasingly more complex. Students with autism eventually became desensitized to the distractions around them and are able to perform the series of steps that allow them to arrive at class on time without having to completely cut out any social interaction along the way.

As with all other modules, it is imperative that Ambassadors anticipate distracting situations that might arise and use their training to refocus the student's attention back on the task at hand. If necessary, it is fine for the Ambassador to improvise, as long as the improvisation falls well within the range of acceptable behavior. Should more assistance be necessary, the Ambassador should not hesitate to engage a teacher or school supervisor.

Organizing
Your Time

An Autism Ambassadors
Original Module

Intro

The purpose of this module is to teach students with autism how to plan and organize their time so they can study for tests, write papers, et cetera without becoming overwhelmed. Organization can be challenging for any teenage student, but students with autism typically have a great deal of difficulty planning their time and completing tasks in a timely fashion. This creates more anxiety for these students as deadlines draw closer and they feel overwhelmed, which only creates further anxiety.

This module takes place in any area of school where there is desk or table; a cafeteria is fine as long as there is not too much eating or other commotion in the background. Likewise, a library is ideal as long as the school's librarians are not so noise-averse that they will not permit Ambassadors and students to discuss what they need to for the purposes of the exercise.

The Ambassador should be seated right next to the student with autism so that the Ambassador can help guide and oversee all of the student's notebook organizing. The student with autism will need her backpack, all of her notebooks, and several worksheets and pages of notes from classes, as well as a physical day planner. Even though most students have smartphones, and most smartphones have day planner apps, those apps tend to be hard to take in and remain hidden on the phone; the better way for a student with autism to process all of her assignments is to have all of them in front of her.

Much of what is required for this module is addressed in our module **Taking Notes in Class;** ideally, this module should be done in conjunction with **Taking Notes in Class, Organizing Notebooks,** and **Making a Plan.**

As with all of our other modules, should the student show signs of extended disengagement or display self-stimulatory behavior with her hands, the Ambassador should refer to our introductory module **Pay**

Attention/Calm Hands in order to get the student to be fully present for the lesson.

We are now ready to begin. The Ambassador and the student with autism enter the work room and sit down at a desk or table.

AMBASSADOR: (Student's name), today we are going to make a plan for all the work and studying you have for the week.

STUDENT: [fidgets]

AMBASSADOR: Remember how we made a plan to go out with friends? Remember how we let them know and figured out a time to get together, and how much fun we had because we planned so well? The same thing is true when it comes to our schoolwork. We have to make a plan to do homework and study for tests.

> Simply telling the student to organize her time, or even simply to write down assignments, is too abstract a concept for the student to process. The Ambassador needs to reference something concrete the student has already learned, preferably something that had a positive payoff, such as the fun the student ended up having by making social plans with her friends.

STUDENT: But schoolwork isn't fun.

AMBASSADOR: I agree. And neither is the part where we have to make a plan. Organization takes a lot of time and hard work. But just like it was fun when you went out with your friends after you made a plan, it will be fun when you get to tell your mom and dad you got an A on a test after you organized your time, right?

STUDENT: [nods]

The Ambassador takes out the day planner and holds it up.

AMBASSADOR: This is your planner. We're going to write everything down in here to help us keep track of your schedule. First, I want you to write down all your afterschool and weekend appointments, and when your family eats dinner every night.

STUDENT: [writes all of it down]

AMBASSADOR: Great; now let's go through all of your classes for tomorrow. Let's start with English. Do you have any assignments due in English?

STUDENT: We have to read Chapter 10 in *Of Mice and Men*.

AMBASSADOR: Okay, how long does it take you to read one chapter?

STUDENT: About an hour.

AMBASSADOR: Great—find a time that works.

STUDENT: [consults the planner] My family eats dinner at 7:00.

AMBASSADOR: Okay, then let's make it 6:00, so you'll be done by 7:00. Let's write that down in your planner. Next, what do you have to do in math?

STUDENT: I have to do 15 problem sets.

AMBASSADOR: How long do you think that will take?

STUDENT: 45 minutes. It usually takes me 3 minutes per problem set, and I have 15 problem sets.

Plenty of students with autism love math and should be encouraged to factor this skill set into the exercise. Ambassadors should explain to them that they are now problem solving in math as well as in their lives.

AMBASSADOR: Okay, how about you do that when you get home from school?

STUDENT: I have karate at 3:30.

The Ambassador is well aware that the student has karate then, but he wants the student to see that for herself and plan around it.

AMBASSADOR: When does karate end, and how long does it take to get home?

Some students with autism have difficulty with two-step questions, such as the one above. For these students, the Ambassador should break the question into two questions.

STUDENT: 4:30, and it takes 15 minutes to get home.

AMBASSADOR: Okay, so if you're home at 4:45, and then have a snack and relax for a half-hour, what time would that be?

STUDENT: 5:15.

AMBASSADOR: And if you spend 45 minutes doing math, what time will that end?

STUDENT: 6:00.

AMBASSADOR: And what do you have at 6:00?

STUDENT: English homework.

AMBASSADOR: Okay, let's write all that down in your planner—English homework, math homework, karate, snack, and meals.

> The student and Ambassador should continue to stack the student's schedule as outlined above, working around extracurricular activities, autism-related therapies, and meal and family time.

AMBASSADOR: Now that we've learned to organize our time for our daily assignments, let's organize our time for other assignments. Do you have any major papers due or tests to study for?

STUDENT: I have a history paper due on Monday.

AMBASSADOR: Okay, what are you writing about?

STUDENT: The Declaration of Independence.

AMBASSADOR: Can you write the paper all in one day, or do you need more time?

STUDENT: I need to check a couple of books out of the library, but I can write the paper in one day. It only has to be five pages.

> The Ambassador should make sure the student includes the length of the paper as well as any research requirements that will be involved. Consult our module **Finding Favorite Books** for additional tips on helping students find books at their school libraries.

AMBASSADOR: Okay, let's check out the books right after lunch so we have them ready. Can you write the paper this weekend?

STUDENT: Yes. We're visiting my grandma on Sunday, but I can work on Saturday.

> Students with autism can have lives that are every bit as programmed as those of their typical peers, and sometimes, if they have autism-related therapies, their time can be even more pressed. Ambassadors should explore the option of working on weekends but should be prepared to help the student find time for all long-term assignments during the week.

AMBASSADOR: Great. Let's write that down in your planner. How about tests?

STUDENT: I have a chemistry test on Friday.

AMBASSADOR: On how many sections?

STUDENT:	Two.
AMBASSADOR:	How much time do you need to study?
STUDENT:	Only an hour and a half, but I won't be home at all on Thursday night because that's when I see all my therapists.
AMBASSADOR:	Okay, then let's make sure we write down some time on Wednesday. I see that Wednesday is wide open. So let's have you study from 8:00 to 9:30, okay?
STUDENT:	Okay.
AMBASSADOR:	Great. Write that down, and good job organizing your time!

Outro

In this module, the Ambassador taught a series of steps that began with helping the student plan a daily schedule. Then the exercise progressed to helping the student understand how to plan over a longer term to write an essay or study for a test. Since the Ambassador will be dealing with the student's belongings (the planner), which can be a touchy subject for students with autism, special care should be taken to avoid creating a situation in which the student reacts adversely to the exercise.

As with all other modules, it is imperative that Ambassadors anticipate distracting situations that might arise and use their training to refocus the student's attention back on the task at hand. If necessary, it is fine for the Ambassador to improvise, as long as the improvisation falls well within the range of acceptable behavior. Should more assistance be necessary, the Ambassador should not hesitate to engage a teacher or school supervisor.

Finding Favorite Books

An Autism Ambassadors Original Module

Intro

The purpose of this module is to teach students how to go to the library and find their favorite books—initially with the help of a librarian, but ultimately without the librarian's help. Library time is an important part of a school day, and as students get older, they will be required to find books to help them with school and research projects. Starting with favorite books is an ideal way to acclimate students with autism to the library environment while also teaching them how to build important research skills that will ultimately help them with all of their future academic endeavors.

The quiet, often austere ambience of libraries can be isolating and disorienting to some students with autism, especially those who require a great deal of reassurance from the presence of either familiar people or familiar objects. Ambassadors might need to employ physical gestures from time to time to reassure their student partners, in lieu of more vocal prompts that would be inappropriate in a library.

This module takes place in the library either during or after school. We will need other students to role-play and take turns being the student with autism, but we will also need help either from the real librarian or a student pretending to the librarian. Student simulators should sit at library tables near the student with autism.

As with all of our other modules, should the student show signs of extended disengagement or display self-stimulatory behavior with his hands, the Ambassador should refer to our introductory module **Pay Attention/Calm Hands** in order to get the student to be fully present for the lesson.

We are now ready to begin.

AMBASSADOR: (Student's name), today we're going to find some of our favorite books in the library.

STUDENT: [sits down, starts playing with hands]

AMBASSADOR: What are some of your favorite books?

> The Ambassador needs to understand that libraries can be overwhelming to students with autism. Given that these students frequently find solace in familiar routines or items, identifying their favorite books can be a way to calm their nerves.

STUDENT: I like trains.

> As with many of our other modules, the student replies with a non sequitur, which is typical of many students with autism, especially when they are uncomfortable or being asked to do something they do not wish to do. The Ambassador should gently address the student's comment; in this case, the Ambassador can use the non sequitur to guide the student back to the subject at hand.

AMBASSADOR: I like trains, too. Right now we're in a library and we need to find a good book. So maybe later on we can find a book about trains if you'd like, okay?

STUDENT: Okay. (names a favorite book)

AMBASSADOR: I like that book, too. Come on, let's go try to find it together.

> The Ambassador needs to be ready to improvise at all times; should the book that the student mentions not be readily available, the Ambassador should suggest another title that she thinks might be familiar and enjoyable to the student.

STUDENT: [starts to whine]

AMBASSADOR: We're in a library. Everyone around us is studying or reading, so let's remember to keep our voices down so we don't disturb them, okay?

> Since the library is an environment that requires extreme quiet, any behavior that involves making noise or distracting other students should be immediately addressed. Additionally, the Ambassador should always remind the student why he needs to be quiet (i.e., that everyone is studying or reading).

AMBASSADOR: [thumbs down a row of books until she finds the title] I don't know where to look; the books are organized by sections and titles. Do you want to ask the librarian to help us?

During early iterations of this exercise, the Ambassador should emphasize the importance of working with the school's librarian and teach the student with autism how the librarian can help him.

STUDENT: [nods]

The Ambassador and the student walk over to the librarian, who looks up.

LIBRARIAN: Hi there. Can I help you?

AMBASSADOR: (Student's name) and I are looking for a book. Can you help us find it?

LIBRARIAN: I'm sure I can. What is the name of the book?

AMBASSADOR: (Student's name), what book do you want the librarian to help you find?

STUDENT: [fidgets]

AMBASSADOR: (Student's name), the librarian wants to help you find the book. But he can't help you find it until you tell him what the name of the book is.

Every time an Ambassador can attach a reason to an action or request, it is helpful to students with autism who may not inherently understand why this step needs to be taken and thus might feel inclined to withdraw.

STUDENT: [names book]

LIBRARIAN: I know where that book is. It will be over in the fiction section.

Middle and high school libraries are frequently organized by the Dewey Decimal System; it's important to emphasize to the student the notion of categories.

AMBASSADOR: Right, because it's a novel. A novel is something that the author wrote out of her imagination. If it were a historical book, it would be in the history section, and if it were a scientific book, it would be in the science section. Thank you!

The Ambassador and student make their way over to the fiction section.

AMBASSADOR: Hmm, the author's last name is (author's name), and the books are organized alphabetically. Do you want to help me look?

STUDENT: [nods]

AMBASSADOR: Great! Let's look for the book.

The Ambassador and student thumb through the book titles on the shelves until they find the one they're looking for.

AMBASSADOR: Great job! You found it! Do you want to find another book?

STUDENT: Yes.

AMBASSADOR: I have an idea: Don't you have a book report due in (name of class) this week?

> The Ambassador should try to ensure that the student searches for a book in a different category; that is, if the last book they found was a work of fiction, then they should look for something in history, science, or another category this time.

STUDENT: [nods]

AMBASSADOR: Okay, what book do you have to do it on?

STUDENT: (names a title)

AMBASSADOR: Great. I know; why don't you find it by yourself this time?

STUDENT: [thumbs down the rows of books until he finds the title]

AMBASSADOR: Great job! You found it!

> To help the student do the book report he needs to do, please refer to our module **Giving an Oral Report in Class.**

Outro

For this module, we started by having the Ambassador turn the library into an inviting atmosphere for the student with autism. Extra consideration for the environment was factored in, and Ambassadors must be aware of the need to maintain a calm demeanor at all times. Once students have learned to find their favorite books, you can use these skills to help them find books they need for research projects for class.

As with all other modules, it is imperative that Ambassadors anticipate distracting situations that might arise and use their training to refocus the student's attention back on the task at hand. If necessary, it is fine for the Ambassador to improvise, as long as the improvisation falls well within the range of acceptable behavior. Should more assistance be necessary, the Ambassador should not hesitate to engage a teacher or the librarian.

Organizing Notebooks

*An Autism Ambassadors
Original Module*

Intro

The purpose of this module is to teach students with autism how to keep their notebooks organized so that they can access the materials they need for each class. Organization can be a challenging task for any teenage student, but students with autism typically have a great deal of difficulty with associative thinking skills; while they might know a great deal about one subject, they will often struggle to connect the dots between that subject and other related subjects. Therefore, a student with autism might not see any distinction between notes taken in American history class and a handout she received in geometry. This module will teach students with autism how to separate their academic materials into groups related to subjects and, then file them into their notebooks so that they can access the materials for their classes as need be.

This module takes place in any area of school where there is desk or table; a cafeteria is fine as long as there is not too much eating or other commotion in the background. Likewise, a library is ideal as long as the school's librarians are not so noise-averse that they will not permit Ambassadors and students to discuss what they need to for the purposes of the exercise. The Ambassador should be seated right next to the student with autism so that the Ambassador can help guide and oversee all of the student's notebook organizing. The student with autism will need her backpack, all of her notebooks, and several worksheets and pages of notes from classes. Much of what is required for this module is addressed in our module **Taking Notes in Class**; ideally, these modules should be done together, with **Taking Notes in Class** preceding **Organizing Notebooks.**

As with all of our other modules, should the student show signs of extended disengagement or display self-stimulatory behavior with her hands, the Ambassador should refer to our introductory module **Pay Attention/Calm Hands** in order to get the student to be fully present for the lesson.

We are now ready to begin. The Ambassador and the student with autism enter the work room and sit down at a desk or table.

AMBASSADOR: (Student's name), today we are going to organize our note-books.

STUDENT: [fidgets]

AMBASSADOR: The reason we organize our notebooks is so we can find what we need when we're in class. Otherwise we might spend time, instead of taking notes while the teacher is talking, flipping through worksheets or notes from the wrong subject.

> Students with autism will sometimes line up objects compulsively; they have terrible anxiety with new or foreign concepts and therefore try to instill order into their lives whenever possible. However, this might not apply to school-related work, and their backpacks will often reflect this. Therefore, as with all of our other modules, it is always a good idea for Ambassadors to explain the reason for the task at hand.

AMBASSADOR: Do you have your backpack?

STUDENT: [nods]

AMBASSADOR: Great. Can I see it?

The student hands over her backpack to the Ambassador, who unzips it and pulls out a mess of notebooks, worksheets, notes, pens, and paper.

AMBASSADOR: I see we have a lot of stuff here. Would you like to help me put everything in order so we can organize our notebooks?

STUDENT: [looks away]

AMBASSADOR: Here; I'll start. First of all, let's put everything into piles. We'll make one pile for math, one for English, and keep on going until we have a pile for every subject.

The Ambassador starts to divide up the materials, but the student starts flapping her hands.

> Many students with autism have significant tactile issues. While the Ambassador is not touching the student, the Ambassador is touching the student's belongings, which might trigger the student's anxiety. The Ambassador should proceed as outlined below, especially if the student's anxiety cannot be quelled.

AMBASSADOR: I see you're upset. Would you like to organize your materials yourself?

STUDENT: Yes.

AMBASSADOR: Okay. Why don't I just sit here and help you out from my side of the desk?

STUDENT: Okay.

AMBASSADOR: First, put all your math work into one pile.

STUDENT: [sorts through all the materials accordingly, until all the math materials are separated out into one pile]

AMBASSADOR: Now let's do the same thing with all of our English materials.

STUDENT: [continues sorting, but places some of the history materials into the English pile]

AMBASSADOR: (Student's name), I don't think that's English, I think that belongs with history.

STUDENT: But it's written in English.

AMBASSADOR: That's an excellent point, but everything is written in English except for our Spanish (or French, etc.) work. So right now let's only put in things that are related to English class.

> The Ambassador should be prepared to discuss the specifics of what is being learned in English class—*The Catcher in the Rye,* et cetera—in order to make more clear associations for the student.

STUDENT: [separates all the materials into piles]

AMBASSADOR: Great job separating your papers! Now let's separate the papers in each pile into notes you took in class and handouts the teacher gave you.

> As with all of our lesson plans, whenever a student with autism does something correctly, the Ambassador should positively reinforce the student's actions.

> While it is ideal for the student to be as organized as possible, the Ambassador should gauge how receptive the student is to the exercise. Should the student become too frustrated, the Ambassador should permit the student to conclude the exercise by simply organizing the materials into piles and placing the piles into a notebook (or several subject-related notebooks).

STUDENT: [separates the papers into notes and handouts]

AMBASSADOR: Great job! Now let's separate everything by date. Let's put the notes you took first at the top, and then keep going all the way to the notes you took last.

STUDENT: [starts organizing notes, but gets confused]

AMBASSADOR: I see that you're getting confused. Let's take a look at the notes and see if we can figure out when they were taken. When did you study the American Revolution?

STUDENT: I think it was September.

AMBASSADOR: I think that's right. And when did you study the Civil War?

STUDENT: I think it was last week.

AMBASSADOR: Great. Then let's put the Civil War papers on top and the American Revolution papers on the bottom.

> For some subjects, like American history and math, the Ambassador can ask these questions based on logical order (e.g., what came first, the American Revolution or the Civil War?) rather than based on the student's recollection.

STUDENT: [follows the Ambassador's directions]

AMBASSADOR: Good job! Now let's put everything into notebooks (or your notebook).

> Younger students might still only have one notebook for all subjects, while older students will almost certainly have a different notebook for each subject. For students who have only one notebook, an additional step involving tab subject dividers should be taken.

STUDENT: [follows the Ambassador's directions]

AMBASSADOR: Good job organizing your notebooks (or notebook)!

Outro

In this module, we taught a series of steps that began with preparation—taking out notebooks, handouts, and any other pertinent materials—and then walked the student through a number of steps until all of her materials were organized by subject and date. Since the Ambassador was dealing with the student's belongings, which can be a touchy subject for students with autism, special consideration was taken in case the student reacted adversely to the exercise.

As with all other modules, it is imperative that Ambassadors anticipate distracting situations that might arise and use their training to refocus the student's attention back on the task at hand. If necessary, it is fine for the Ambassador to improvise, as long as the improvisation falls well within the range of acceptable behavior. Should more assistance be necessary, the Ambassador should not hesitate to engage a teacher or school supervisor.

Study Hall

*An Autism Ambassadors
Original Module*

Intro

The purpose of this module is to get students to sit quietly and engage in appropriate activities during study hall, while simultaneously building friendships in a structured and safe environment. Study hall, a typical part of a middle school student's daily experience, can be also referred to as silent reading time, circle time, or free time (depending on the age of the student). There can be expectations and confusions on the part of teachers and other adults that students with autism know how to work by themselves during study hall. There are a myriad of ways that a school can organize students' free time. Usually, however, study hall is relatively unstructured, allows for students to choose their activities, and encourages students to use their time productively. Our curriculum categories teach all of these skills; however, this module focuses specifically on teaching students how to choose their activities and make good use of their time.

This module takes place at the student's desk in school. Schools will often assign a specific desk to each student. To simulate this situation, you can use a sharpie to mark a letter or a number on a piece of paper and then tape it on the desk or chair. In our exercise, we have put a felt *A* on the desk where we want the student to sit. To replicate a classroom setting, we need other students, which we will select from among the students in Ambassador training. All Ambassador trainees role-play and take turns being the student who needs assistance. Student simulators will sit at desks near the student with autism, while another student will sit in the teacher's chair and play the teacher. In your modeling of this situation, if a different student has taken the seat assigned to the student with autism, prompt the student with autism to politely ask the typical student to move.

As with all of our other modules, should the student show signs of extended disengagement or display self-stimulatory behavior with his hands, the Ambassador should refer to our introductory module **Pay Attention/Calm Hands** in order to get the student to be fully present for the lesson.

We are now ready to begin.

AMBASSADOR: It's time for study hall; let's find your desk and sit down.

The Ambassador helps the student find his seat so as not to delay the class from beginning and to make sure the transition goes smoothly. If possible, the Ambassador will gently physically guide the student by placing her hand on the student's back.

> It is important to remember that Autism Ambassadors is for students who enjoy helping others and who typically have done some sort of volunteer work in the past, either with their families or with organizations for community service. Ambassadors also typically do not need regular academic assistance and therefore can afford to spend one study hall period a week helping improve another student's life.

AMBASSADOR: Here's your desk, (student's name).

STUDENT: [somewhat confused that there isn't a worksheet or activity already at the desk, as is the case in other classes, begins to make noise]

Paying no attention to the noise, the Ambassador walks over to an area filled with books and brings the student a book (or another piece of work-related material).

AMBASSADOR: [in a loud and firm voice] It's study hall! It's time to read.

STUDENT: [continues to whine, does not open the book]

AMBASSADOR: Try reading, try turning the pages and see what you might like. (Note: Ambassadors should pick a book that has photographs and caption information that a student with autism might find interesting regardless of his academic interests and abilities.)

STUDENT: [begins to turn the pages with the Ambassador]

> It is extremely important for Ambassadors not to take personally any feedback from the students with whom they are working; the students' intent is never to hurt the Ambassador's feelings or to be difficult. It is imperative that Ambassadors persevere and not give up, as this process will more than likely take quite some time and practice.

AMBASSADOR: [whispering in the student's ear] You are doing a great job of reading to yourself.

> Having the Ambassador whisper to the student in this situation is important, because the Ambassador needs to get the student's attention. Often, a teacher will move around a room and will lean over a student working and whisper so as not to disturb the entire classroom. Students with

autism need to become accustomed to this behavior. Ambassadors also need to emphasize whispering, because this tone of voice promotes an atmosphere of silence and listening. Whispering also enables Ambassadors to correct students' behavior discreetly, and it is imperative that Ambassadors NEVER embarrass or humiliate students with autism.

STUDENT: [finishes reading book and slowly begins to tap on the desk, disturbing other students]

AMBASSADOR: [directing the student to find something else to do] Looks like you are ready for another activity. What would you like to do?

STUDENT: [does not respond]

The student may not respond for a myriad of reasons ranging from fear of getting the answer wrong to not understanding to having little verbal language. Ambassador training should include what the potential reasons are.

AMBASSADOR: I know; let's look in your backpack, and see what your homework is.

The Ambassador helps the student take out assignment sheets and books from his backpack.

The student may feel disorganized, not know where to start, and/or lack a sense of priority for what homework should come first. He may need help figuring out homework instructions.

AMBASSADOR: Looks like you have math to do. Let's take it out and see what we have, and I will help get you started.

STUDENT: [appears unable to sit still]

The student may want to sit still and comply, but may have a hard time doing so and may not have the patience to wait while the Ambassador figures out what the homework requires the student to do.

AMBASSADOR: [noticing that the student is having difficulty, tries to hurry and begins to narrate what she is reading] Wow, this is going to be a little hard but also a little fun. Let's get your homework done so that you will have less to do at home.

STUDENT: I don't want to do this now.

It is important for the Ambassador to ignore difficult behavior and instead to redirect by saying something like, "Hey let's do the first example together." Should there be further difficulty, Ambassadors can always reach out to a teacher. At times Ambassadors might need to pick a different subject to work on.

AMBASSADOR: [offers two different pencils to work with and immediately begins explaining the problem through a combination of showing and narrating]

The Ambassador's behavior enables the student to understand what to do. This makes the student more receptive.

STUDENT: [less anxious, smiling] I can do it myself.

Outro

In this module, we started by teaching our Ambassadors to get a book to look through with the student. When the students were finished reading, we introduced the concept of taking out the backpack and doing homework so that when the student is at home, he will have less homework to do alone. As we mentioned in the learning moments, this will not come easily to students with autism, nor will it come easily to the Ambassadors. However, over the course of time and with increased experience in study hall, the skills to keep themselves occupied will be presented enough times so that students with autism will be able to occupy themselves and not be disruptive to other students who are trying to work.

Finally, although getting homework done is a study hall objective for most students, given the challenges faced by students with autism, they may also choose to spend their time doing projects or completing work that was too difficult for them to complete in class. As with all other modules, it is imperative that Ambassadors anticipate distracting situations that might arise and use their training to refocus the student's attention back on the task at hand. If necessary, it is fine for the Ambassador to improvise, as long as the improvisation falls well within the range of acceptable behavior. Should more assistance be necessary, the Ambassador should not hesitate to engage a teacher or school supervisor.

SECTION 4

Outing/ Extracurricular Modules

Students of all ages go on numerous class trips during school hours as a means of supplementing their academic studies with real world examples of the kinds of subjects they are studying. Although these trips are typically a source of great enjoyment for students, as the trips provide a respite from class time, they can rapidly devolve into a nightmare due to the manifold possibilities for a student with autism to create a disruption that distracts the class from the subject at hand. The modules in this section teach Ambassadors how to anticipate and react to a wide range of external stimuli so that class trips run as smoothly as possible. There is also one module that has nothing to do with a class trip but instead teaches an extracurricular skill set that can be of tremendous emotional and financial benefit to the student with autism.

The modules that make up this section are as follows:

1. Riding the Bus

2. Class Trip/Museum

3. Class Trip/Zoo

4. Interviewing for a High School Job

Riding the Bus teaches the most important underlying skill set a student with autism will need in order to successfully attend, and participate in, a field trip—namely, behaving in a socially appropriate manner while en route from the school to the destination of the class. Because bus trips provide a plethora of potential distractions by way of unfamiliar external stimuli, Ambassadors teach desensitization and redirection to students, who will face a veritable barrage of distractions that could, if the student acts out, prove dangerous to the safety of the class.

Class Trip/Museum addresses the importance of decorum in one of the most decorum-heavy environments in which students might find themselves: a museum. Students with autism might find the silence and austerity of the museum off-putting, or they might wish to touch the artwork, which, without proper anticipation and/or intervention from an Ambassador, could create a challenging situation for the tour guide, the teacher, and the other students. This exercise teaches Ambassadors how to apply extensive redirection techniques that can not only keep the student with autism focused on the task at hand but can also allow her to gain a great deal from the class trip.

Class Trip/Zoo adds a very important element of potential danger to the set of circumstances outlined above. While zoos are on the opposite end of the spectrum from museums as far as decorum and any required behavior is concerned, they are laden with pitfalls and dangerous possibilities of which Ambassadors must be aware at all times. More than any of our other modules, this module emphasizes the need for the Ambassador to have a faculty member close at hand and encourages Ambassadors not to act if they feel overwhelmed by the situation.

Interviewing for a High School Job recognizes that students with autism can be valuable additions to the work force in several high school job–friendly work environments, such as ice cream parlors and fast food restaurants. Not only is working at a job a self-esteem boost for students (both typical and those with autism), it also can provide some much-needed revenue for the student's family, who will most likely have had a significant strain placed on their finances resulting from their child's condition. In this module, Ambassadors role-play the boss interviewing the student with autism and prepare the student for the types of questions and challenges (filling out a job application, for starters) that the student is likely to face.

Riding the Bus

*An Autism Ambassadors
Original Module*

Intro

The purpose of this lesson is to get students with autism to engage in appropriate behavior while on the bus en route to a class trip; this is a common occurrence for schoolchildren of all ages. Class trips often involve long bus trips from school to a destination, during which students with autism might become scared and/or disoriented and act inappropriately. Not only is this distracting for the other students, it is potentially dangerous for the bus driver, whose undivided attention must be on the road.

The module will simulate an actual school bus setting, with desks lined up in rows to represent bus seats, and a tape recorder or CD player present to provide background road noise (e.g., honking horns, external car engines, etc.). Often, students are given assigned seats on bus trips; to simulate this situation, you can use a sharpie to mark a letter or a number on a piece of paper and then tape it on the desk or chair at which the student with autism is to sit. In our exercise, we have put a felt *A* on this bus seat.

We will require other students to role-play everything from the student with autism to the other students on the bus. The student simulators will sit at seats near the student with autism while the Ambassador will sit in a seat next to the student with autism.

As with all of our other modules, should the student show signs of extended disengagement or display self-stimulatory behavior with her hands, the Ambassador should refer to our introductory module **Pay Attention/Calm Hands** in order to get the student to be fully present for the lesson.

We are now ready to begin. The Ambassador leads the student with autism over to her seat.

AMBASSADOR: Welcome to the bus, (student's name). Here's your seat, (student's name).

STUDENT: [flaps hands, resists being led over to seat]

> It is important for Ambassadors to remember that the more external stimulation to which a student with autism is exposed, the more likely that student is to react with self-stimulatory behavior, like flapping or noise-making. Ambassadors must not pay any attention to the behavior, but rather continue to redirect the student with autism toward the task at hand.

AMBASSADOR: [paying no attention to the student's flapping, continues to walk student over to the seat and repeats] Here's your seat, (student's name).

STUDENT: [still whining, sits down]

AMBASSADOR: Great job sitting down! Now let's get ready for the bus trip.

> Whenever a student does an assigned task, it is extremely important for the Ambassador to compliment the student and positively reinforce her actions, no matter how mundane the action seems.

AMBASSADOR: Our class is going on a class trip today. We're going to (the museum, the planetarium, etc.).

STUDENT: [looks around the bus nervously]

AMBASSADOR: Have you ever been to (the museum, the planetarium, etc.) before?

STUDENT: I like trains. I want to go on the train.

> Students with autism frequently speak in non sequiturs and perseverate, or focus single-mindedly, on objects like trains, especially when they are feeling socially anxious. And when dealing with matters in which transportation is involved, as is the case here, a student might want to change the subject to something more familiar to her. The Ambassador should be ready for any such detours and be prepared to redirect the conversation back to the topic at hand.

AMBASSADOR: I like trains, too, but we can't take a train to where we're going. In order to get where we need to go, we need to take the bus.

STUDENT: I want to drive my car there.

AMBASSADOR: That would be nice, but there are too many people in our class to drive.

STUDENT: How come?

AMBASSADOR: Well, how many people can fit in your car?

STUDENT: A lot.

AMBASSADOR: I'm sure it's a lot. But how many exactly?

STUDENT: Seven.

AMBASSADOR: Right. But how many people are we taking today?

> Counting is an excellent technique to calm down students with autism. We used it in our **Pay Attention/Calm Hands** module to keep students focused during an unpleasant task, but here we can use it to distract them from perseverating (obsessing) on their unrealistic desire to take the car to the museum.

STUDENT: About 30.

AMBASSADOR: Right. And how many people does your car hold?

STUDENT: Seven.

AMBASSADOR: So we can't take your car, can we?

STUDENT: [shakes her head]

> It is important for the Ambassador to walk the student through the steps, on the order of what is outlined above, so the student can arrive at this conclusion by herself. Additionally, it is important for the Ambassador to emphasize the group nature of the activity, so the student understands that she is part of something larger than herself.

AMBASSADOR: We're all going together, with the rest of the class. And today we're going to (the museum, the planetarium, etc.). Have you ever been there?

STUDENT: [shakes her head]

AMBASSADOR: I have. I love it there. Last time I was there I learned a lot and had a lot of fun, too.

> As with many of our other modules, Ambassadors should always make a point of expressing their enthusiasm for the activity at hand and should reference any past or recent experience they have had.

We hear a loud HONK of a car from the CD player/tape recorder.

STUDENT: [starts to flap nervously]

AMBASSADOR: Oh, there's another car outside! I wonder where they're going today?

> Whenever the student with autism is distracted by outside noise or actions, it is a good idea for the Ambassador to factor the noise or actions into the dialogue. The point is to make the trip as familiar and unthreatening as possible.

AMBASSADOR: Do you think they're going on a field trip, too?

STUDENT: [shakes her head]

AMBASSADOR: Me neither. I think they're probably going somewhere else today.

A couple of other kids start to horse around on the bus. The student with autism starts to copy them.

AMBASSADOR: (Student's name), look outside. Let's count the number of big buildings we see on the way to the field trip.

> Whenever a student with autism is tempted to mimic bad behavior, it is important for the Ambassador to deflect the student's attention to something constructive, like taking note of her surroundings, or opening up a manual about the field trip destination. Again, counting is a time-tested focus tool for students with autism.

The Ambassador and student continue to count buildings until the bus comes to a stop.

AMBASSADOR: You did it! We're here!

Outro

The objective of this module was to desensitize students with autism to long bus rides through frequently unfamiliar neighborhoods so they don't disrupt the environment or distract the driver. For this lesson, we taught Ambassadors how to fit the potential distractions of the school bus environment into the dialogue to ease the anxiety of the student with autism. We also taught Ambassadors to do everything they could to familiarize the student with where the field trip was taking place.

As with all other modules, it is imperative that Ambassadors anticipate distracting situations that might arise and use their training to refocus the student's attention back on the task at hand. Given the potential for hazard in this setting, the Ambassador should be ready to have a teacher or adult supervisor intervene should the student's behavior become especially problematic.

Class Trip/Museum

An Autism Ambassadors
Original Module

Intro

The purpose of this module is to get students to engage in appropriate behavior while out with their class on a trip to a museum, which is a frequent occurrence for students ranging from kindergartners to seniors in high school.

Class trips to museums often involve long stretches of time during which students must stand and pay attention to a tour guide or go from one exhibit to another, during which time students with autism might become disoriented or distracted easily. This behavior can challenge the guide's ability to conduct the tour and also impact the overall experience for the rest of the class. Additionally, if a student misbehaves, he will spend all of his time being tended to instead of enjoying, and learning from, the class trip.

This module will recreate a museum setting, with objects placed around the room to represent exhibits and paintings. We will require other students to role-play everything from the student with autism to the other students on the trip to the guide or docent leading the group tour. Student simulators will stand at spots near the student with autism, a tour guide will stand at the front of the group and address them, and the Ambassador will stand next to the student with autism as the group moves around the museum.

As with all of our other modules, should the student show signs of extended disengagement or display self-stimulatory behavior with his hands, the Ambassador should refer to our introductory module **Pay Attention/Calm Hands** in order to get the student to be fully present for the lesson.

We are now ready to begin. The Ambassador leads the student with autism into the museum.

AMBASSADOR: Welcome to the museum, (student's name).

STUDENT: [looks around nervously, starts to whine and make clucking sounds]

AMBASSADOR: Have you ever been to a museum before? They have lots of terrific paintings and sculptures here by some of the most famous artists in history.

> Even if the student with autism has been to a museum before, it is a good idea for the Ambassador to explain the details of the museum in order to better acclimate the student to this new location. This will cut down on some of the anxiety the student might be feeling as the result of being out of his school or home environment.

AMBASSADOR: Our tour guide is going to lead us on a tour of the museum. We are going to go from room to room and learn about different styles of painting and sculpture.

> Students with autism frequently experience high levels of anxiety when faced with unfamiliar settings. Even though the tour guide will be providing the students with specific details throughout the tour, the Ambassador should do anything in her power to provide as much information as possible to the student with autism beforehand, in order to make the experience feel as familiar as possible. Ambassadors are strongly encouraged to read about the museum tour and learn as much as possible prior to the class field trip.

The tour guide leads the group around the museum and addresses the students at normal volume.

TOUR GUIDE: Hello, students! Today we're going to be looking at some wonderful paintings and sculptures. We are going to start in the (name of painting style or period) wing.

> It is important for the Ambassador to use anything she can to keep the student with autism focused on the task at hand. While ideally the student with autism will be able to follow the tour guide and keep up with the group, the Ambassador should be ready to redirect the student's attention to the many sights of the museum and be ready to break from the pack if necessary.

STUDENT: [walks over to a painting and looks like he is about to touch it]

AMBASSADOR: [walks over to the student and gently taps him on the shoulder] (Student's name), we don't touch the art work here. Back in class we can look at a picture of the painting in a book, and we can touch the painting there, but we can't do it here.

Many students with autism have serious tactile issues as well and love to touch things. Ambassadors need to be aware of this and be prepared to redirect the student at a moment's notice. However, in a similar vein, physical contact is a very sensitive topic for Ambassadors, as it is for everyone who works or takes part in a school environment. It is important to note that, should a student with autism be in danger of actually damaging a painting or sculpture in a museum, the first step should be to gently touch the student's shoulder. Should that not work, the Ambassador should get an adult teacher immediately.

STUDENT: [whines, makes noises]

AMBASSADOR: I know! Let's follow the rest of the students over to that sculpture (or painting)! I'll bet that one's going to be a lot of fun to look at!

The Ambassador should remind the student, should the student have tactile issues with the paintings and/or sculptures, that the artwork will be a lot of fun to LOOK at, as opposed to touch or interact with.

STUDENT: [continues to whine]

AMBASSADOR: Okay, what are some of your favorite shows on TV?

STUDENT: Cartoons.

AMBASSADOR: Me, too. You know what? There are lots of drawings in the museum that are just like cartoons.

The Ambassador is trying to guide the student away from his pressing need to touch the painting. Instead, the Ambassador is trying to get the student to focus on the idea of looking at things by making positive associations to the kinds of things the student watches in his own life.

AMBASSADOR: I know! Why don't we go follow the class and go look at them?

STUDENT: [stops whining and watches the students as they make their way over to another exhibit; follows them]

AMBASSADOR: Great job! Isn't this a terrific place to visit?

STUDENT: Yes.

Outro

The objective of this module was to desensitize students with autism to the considerable challenges of participating in a class trip to the museum, so both they and the other students can get the most out of the experience. For this lesson, we taught Ambassadors how to factor external sights and sounds into the dialogue and keep the student focused on the museum's attractions. Ambassadors need to understand, however, that if the student with autism cannot keep up with the tour, he can still be a part of the field trip without causing any disruption.

As with all other modules, it is imperative that Ambassadors anticipate distracting situations that might arise and use their training to refocus the student's attention back on the task at hand. If necessary, it is fine for the Ambassador to improvise, as long as the improvisation falls well within the range of acceptable behavior. Should more assistance be necessary, the Ambassador should not hesitate to engage a teacher or parent supervisor.

Class Trip/Zoo

*An Autism Ambassadors
Original Module*

Intro

The purpose of this module is to get students to engage in appropriate behavior while on a class outing to a zoo, which is a standard outing for younger students. Class trips to the zoo involve a great deal of walking around an environment that is not only expansive and loud, it is also potentially hazardous. This can pose a great number of challenges both for students with autism and their Ambassadors. Should the tour be a guided one, the student with autism might act out and become distracted easily. This behavior can challenge the guide's ability to conduct the tour and impact the overall experience for the rest of the class.

Additionally, there is the possibility that a student with autism might wander off and get lost, and since most zoos are large places with dangerous possibilities (e.g., lion and gorilla enclosures, water exhibits with seals and otters, etc.), the Ambassador must be aware where the student with autism is at all times and ensure that the student is interacting in a positive, safe manner with the surrounding environment.

This module will recreate a zoo setting, with objects (either pictures of animals or actual plastic animals) placed around the room to represent features one might expect to find at a zoo. A CD player or tape recorder should be playing animal noises to simulate actual noises that students would expect to hear at the zoo.

We will require other students to role-play everything from the student with autism to the other students on the trip to a tour guide. The student simulators will stand at spots near the student with autism, the tour guide will stand at the front of the group and address them, and the Ambassador will stand next to the student with autism.

As with all of our other modules, should the student show signs of extended disengagement or display self-stimulatory behavior with her hands, the Ambassador should refer to our introductory module **Pay Attention/Calm Hands** in order to get the student to be fully present for the lesson.

We are now ready to begin. The Ambassador leads the student with autism into the zoo. The tour guide leads the group around the zoo and addresses the students at normal volume with the animal noises in the background.

TOUR GUIDE: Hello, students! Welcome to the zoo. Today we're going to walk around and see all of the zoo's fascinating animals from all over the world.

STUDENT: [looks around, seemingly disoriented]

> If the student cannot keep up with the group, or be engaged by the tour guide, the Ambassador should be ready to redirect the student's attention to the many sights of the zoo, especially toward some of the student's favorite animals, if the student with autism is able to express what they are.

AMBASSADOR: We're at the zoo now, (student's name). We hear some faraway bird noises.

STUDENT: [looks around and makes monkey sounds]

AMBASSADOR: I hear birds. Today we are going to be seeing all the animals at the zoo, and that includes birds.

> It is important for the Ambassador to use anything he can to keep the student with autism focused. While in many cases the Ambassador would put distracting outside noises on extinction (in essence, ignoring them), here the Ambassador sees an opportunity to work the outside noise into the conversation while redirecting the student's focus back to the task at hand.

AMBASSADOR: I like birds, but I like lots of other animals at the zoo. What are some of your favorite animals?

STUDENT: I like airplanes.

> As we discuss in our module, **Making a Plan,** students with autism frequently speak in non sequiturs, especially when they are excited or anxious. A trip to the zoo has the capability to be overwhelming, so Ambassadors should anticipate such turns in the conversation.

AMBASSADOR: I like airplanes, too. But we're at the zoo, so I would really like to know what some of your favorite animals are, since we came to the zoo to see animals.

STUDENT: I like monkeys. Oh, look! I see the monkey cage! [student walks over to a monkey cage and is about to reach inside the bars]

AMBASSADOR: Walks over to the student and gently taps her on the shoulder. (Student's name), we can't touch the animals here.

> As addressed in our other module, **Class Trip/Museum,** students with autism frequently have tactile issues and like to touch things they should not touch. Additionally, physical contact is a very sensitive topic, as it is in any school environment. It is important to note that, should a student with autism put herself in a position of actual danger at a zoo, the Ambassador should seek assistance from an adult teacher immediately.

STUDENT: [whines, makes noises]

AMBASSADOR: This is a zoo, and these animals aren't friendly. They're not the same as a dog or a cat. But we can look at them all we want.

STUDENT: [grows increasingly frustrated]

AMBASSADOR: Can you tell me some of the things you love to look at, but not touch?

> As we mentioned in our **Class Trip/Museum** module, the Ambassador needs to reinforce the idea of enjoying things by looking, but not touching, and the best way to do this is to remind the student about things in her own life that fit this description.

STUDENT: Cartoons on TV.

AMBASSADOR: That's a great example! Think of the animals exactly the same way you would think about cartoons on TV: You can look all you want, but you cannot touch them.

STUDENT: [stops whining]

AMBASSADOR: What are some of your other favorite animals?

STUDENT: I like monkeys.

AMBASSADOR: I like monkeys, too. But what are some of your other favorite animals?

> It is a good idea to phrase the question this way—what are some of your *other* favorite animals?—should the student be having an especially difficult time disengaging from the animal she wants to touch, which is clearly the case here. The Ambassador should also reinforce that he, too, likes what the student likes before changing the topic back to the more relevant point. As we have discussed in other modules, positive reinforcement is crucial when engaging with students with autism, especially whenever they are in foreign or overstimulating environments such as zoos.

STUDENT: [flaps hands]

AMBASSADOR: Do you like giraffes?

> The Ambassador should be prepared to list animals in the zoo until he comes to one the student likes.

STUDENT: I like giraffes.

AMBASSADOR: Great! Let's go over to (or follow the rest of the students over to) the giraffes!

STUDENT: [stops complaining and follows the Ambassador and/or the other students over to another exhibit]

Outro

The objective of this module was to desensitize students with autism to the considerable challenges of participating in a class outing to the zoo and focus in particular on the issue of safety. For this lesson, we taught Ambassadors how to factor external sights into the dialogue and understand that if the student with autism cannot keep up with the tour, she can still be a part of the activity without causing any disruption.

As with all other modules, it is imperative that Ambassadors anticipate distracting situations that might arise and use their training to refocus the student's attention back on the task at hand. If necessary, it is fine for the Ambassador to improvise, as long as the improvisation falls well within the range of acceptable behavior. Should more assistance be necessary, the Ambassador should not hesitate to engage a teacher or school supervisor.

Interviewing for a High School Job

An Autism Ambassadors Original Module

Intro

The purpose of this module is to teach students how to apply for, and perform the duties of, a typical high school job, such as working in an ice cream or fast food store. Many families who have students with autism face considerable financial strain from the services the student requires, and while not every student with autism can perform the duties of a job, many can with the right training and approach. This can thus potentially offset some of the financial burden on the student's family as well as give the student the kind of well-deserved boost of self-esteem that invariably comes with performing the tasks required for having a job.

This module takes place in the classroom in school; to replicate a work setting, we need other students, which we will select from among the students in Ambassador training. All Ambassador trainees role-play and take turns being the student who needs assistance as well as milling about and playing customers and/or workers in the background.

As with all of our other modules, should the student show signs of extended disengagement or display self-stimulatory behavior with his hands, the Ambassador should refer to our introductory module **Pay Attention/Calm Hands** in order to get the student to be fully present for the lesson.

We are now ready to begin. The Ambassador leads the student with autism over to a desk, which will be used to simulate the interview area.

AMBASSADOR: (Student's name), today we're going to learn how apply for a job. Lots of kids have jobs after school. It's a great way to earn extra money and learn important work skills.

STUDENT: [sits and fidgets]

AMBASSADOR: I have a job. I work in (names her job).

Should the Ambassador not have a job, she should make a point to discuss any internship or other volunteer duties—short of this one—she has ever performed. Any position as a camp counselor, Big Brother, or afterschool tutor is acceptable.

AMBASSADOR: So today I'm going to pretend to interview you. Pretending to do something is a great way to prepare, just like practicing basketball is a great way to become a much better basketball player in games.

STUDENT: I like basketball.

AMBASSADOR: I like basketball, too. And I like working and making money. And I think you're going to like it, too. So today I'm going to pretend to be the owner of an ice cream store and I'm going to pretend to interview you. Do you like ice cream?

STUDENT: [nods]

Although this is a popular job, many students with autism have severe gluten and casein allergies and have been on restricted diets for their entire lives. Ambassadors should be sensitive to this and should be ready to switch to any one of a plethora of other options (fast food, retail stores, etc.).

AMBASSADOR: Great. So today we're going to do a pretend job interview. I'm going to ask you questions about yourself that will let me understand why I should hire you to work for me.

Most jobs require applicants to fill out a form; should the student be unable to perform this on his own, the Ambassador should help the student understand concepts like filling out address, work history, et cetera.

AMBASSADOR: Have you ever had a job before?

STUDENT: [gets distracted by something in the background]

AMBASSADOR: I know that you're interested in what is happening inside the store, but there will be plenty of time for that once you start working. Have you ever had a job before?

STUDENT: No.

AMBASSADOR: Do you ever help out with chores around your house?

STUDENT: [nods]

AMBASSADOR: Why don't you tell me some of the work you do in your house to help out your mom, dad, and brothers and sisters?

The Ambassador should use this question as a prompt to encourage the student to list tasks he does around the house analogous to any duties that might be required of him at the job. But since it will be impossible to improvise and analogize every stage of a potential job, the Ambassador should do her best to make basic comparisons such as the one below.

STUDENT: I wash the dishes and put away the laundry.

AMBASSADOR: Great! At this job you'll have to wash ice cream scoopers, which is just like washing dishes. And you'll have to carry ice cream canisters back and forth from the freezer, which is just like putting away laundry. Can you do that?

STUDENT: Yes, I can do that.

AMBASSADOR: Great, then you should have no problem doing those tasks at work. Now do you have transportation to work and back home?

STUDENT: I like trains.

Students with autism frequently perseverate, or focus single-mindedly, on objects like trains. If the question concerns transportation, and the student answers with something on the order of the above response, the Ambassador should be ready to redirect the student back to the topic at hand.

AMBASSADOR: I like trains, too, but I don't think we should talk about them during our job interview.

STUDENT: Why not?

AMBASSADOR: Well, can you take a train to the ice cream store?

STUDENT: No.

AMBASSADOR: I don't think so either. But we can discuss transportation to and from work. Is there any other way you can get to work if you get this job?

STUDENT: [depending on the transportation options available to the student] I can take the bus (or I can walk, or my mom or dad can take me).

AMBASSADOR: Great answer! Are you excited to get a job?

STUDENT: Yes.

AMBASSADOR: Can you tell me some of the reasons why?

STUDENT: I want to work hard like I do around my house and make money.

AMBASSADOR: Great answer! You got the job! Be prepared to start next week.

STUDENT: Okay.

Outro

The objective of this module was to desensitize students with autism to the pressures of applying for the types of afterschool jobs suited for high school students. For this lesson, we taught the student how to walk through the various stages of job interviews, factoring in background noises and action that might prove to be a distraction for students with autism. As stated earlier, Ambassadors should use the basic principles of this module as a means to explore a number of other employment options, such as department stores, stockrooms, and fast food restaurants.

As with all other modules, it is imperative that Ambassadors anticipate distracting situations that might arise and use their training to refocus the student's attention back on the task at hand. If necessary, it is fine for the Ambassador to improvise, as long as the improvisation falls well within the range of acceptable behavior. Should more assistance be necessary, the Ambassador should not hesitate to engage a teacher or school supervisor.

Social Situations Modules

Whitehile the modules in this section generally address social issues related to school, the underlying skill sets they cover speak to the kinds of shortcomings present in nearly all students with autism: namely, their inability to process social cues the way typical students can. Outwardly, many students with autism appear indifferent to the social morays of their peers, but inwardly, many are acutely aware that they don't fit in, and this causes them tremendous pain and consternation. While, technically speaking, students with autism have to learn these cues with a part of their brains not hardwired for these tasks, they can still be taught a behavioral approach to basic socializing in a school environment that can provide them with the tools to have a rewarding social life.

The ten modules that make up this section are as follows:

1. Asking Someone Out on a Date

2. Cafeteria Etiquette

3. Cursing and Offensive Language

4. Explaining Your Diagnosis to Friends

5. Finding Friends at Lunch

6. Finding Favorite Popular Music

7. Joining a Club at School

8. Making a Plan

9. School Dance

Asking Someone Out on a Date uses a two-scenario structure to teach students not only how to ask someone out on a date but also how to tell when that person is just being polite and does not really want to go. The

Ambassador then contrasts the unsuccessful date proposal with a successful one that involves flexibility on the part of the student to make a plan that works for both parties.

Cafeteria Etiquette teaches students with autism, many of whom do not place a high priority on their eating habits, how to sit at a cafeteria table with their peers without drawing attention to themselves. While this might strike some as a lower level skill set, many Ambassadors have reported that they are surprised at the level of seeming indifference their peers with autism display for socially acceptable table manners. Ambassadors need to anticipate that they might attain only a moderate level of success, and should arm themselves with a healthy supply of plastic forks and knives and napkins.

Cursing and Offensive Language is an especially touchy subject in an era not only of political correctness but also in which denigrating the wrong ethnic or religious group might actually become a safety hazard. Students with autism often lack the filter to keep their thoughts to themselves, and thus Ambassadors are taught a technique to make up for this lack with a mechanism that redirects the students' thoughts toward something more constructive. As they were in our **Finding Favorite Books** module, Ambassadors need to be especially sensitive to the volume of their student partners' voices, as much of the language covered should be spoken as quietly as possible.

Explaining Your Diagnosis to Friends teaches students with autism how to be out in the open about their disability by discussing it with their peers. Ownership is the key to empowerment, and one of the problems faced by many students with autism is their inherent feelings of disempowerment. Due in large part to the ever-expanding influx of students with autism, school environments everywhere are working to creating a more inclusive and nurturing environment for these students, a movement in which all students should play an active role.

Finding Friends at Lunch teaches students with autism how to navigate the busy social beehive of the cafeteria and find a group of friends with whom to sit. While they are friends and serviceable anchors to students with autism, Ambassadors have schedules and other obligations of their own and thus cannot be expected to be available at all times to their students. This module teaches students with autism how to fight their natural tendencies to sit alone and instead make their lunch hours a fun and social experience for all.

Finding Favorite Popular Music addresses one of the most pressing contemporary topics of conversation among school-aged children—namely popular music. With scripted television shows about music seemingly filling the few spots not already inhabited by music talent shows, and with what seems like a new form of music-serving technology being developed by technology companies on a near-weekly basis, today's students are barraged by popular music and are expected to be conversant in everything from *American Idol* to Spotify. This module teaches students with autism how to orient themselves in this direction and, if they are not already proficient on the technological side (which, given their natural inclinations, they very well might be), how to download and share online music.

Joining a Club at School explores the arena of school clubs, an arena that can seem overwhelming to many students (especially freshmen), but can be downright daunting to students with autism. Joining a club is an extremely important component of any student's social life, and a student with autism, who might be fighting her instincts to avoid being a part of anything, needs to learn the skills involved in not only determining which clubs she wishes to join, but also how to become part of the club's activities and befriend its members.

Making a Plan teaches students with autism how to ask other students out—not on dates, but rather on social engagements. Even if it's as simple as a trip to the mall, students with autism typically feel too inhibited to initiate social contact, even with their fellow students with whom they might feel comfortable. This module outlines the steps that a student with autism should take to ensure that his social calendar remains filled with satisfying social outings and teaches him how to organize a calendar as well.

School Dance addresses the challenges of a Saturday night school dance. This is invariably a social and potentially romantic opportunity for most typical students, but it is a cornucopia of potential pitfalls for students with autism. The combination of social milieu, blasting music, and blinding lights can be a perfect storm of terror for students with autism, but this module breaks them down into a series of easily accessible baby steps that incrementally desensitize the student to what she will be dealing with at the dance.

Asking Someone Out on a Date

*An Autism Ambassadors
Original Module*

Intro

The objective of this module is to teach students with autism to initiate a plan for a date and react appropriately if the other person is politely trying to turn the student down. Asking peers to go out on a date can be daunting for typical students, let alone students with autism. Teaching students with autism appropriate responses and questions involves a great deal of planning and anticipation; note that unlike other modules, this module covers two situations: In one, the student with autism asks the Ambassador out on a date and is politely deflected; in the other, the student asks the Ambassador out and is not rejected, so a plan must be made.

This module takes place in a hallway setting in school; to replicate a hallway setting, we need other students, which we will select from among the students in Ambassador training. All Ambassador trainees role-play and take turns being the student who needs assistance as well as other members of the class milling about.

As with all of our other modules, should the student show signs of extended disengagement or display self-stimulatory behavior with his hands, the Ambassador should refer to our introductory module **Pay Attention/Calm Hands** in order to get the student to be fully present for the lesson.

We are now ready to begin.

Situation One:

AMBASSADOR: Okay, (student's name), today we're going to pretend that you're asking me out on a date.

STUDENT: Okay.

AMBASSADOR: We're going to do this two times. The first time I want you to try to guess how I'm feeling about you asking me out, okay? Then we'll do the same thing the second time, but I'm going to be acting differently.

STUDENT: Okay.

The Ambassador gives the student a heads-up that they will be doing the module twice but does not want to tip her hand too much, because she wants to see how well the student catches on.

STUDENT: Hi, (Ambassador's name). What's up?

AMBASSADOR: Not much.

STUDENT: I was wondering what you were doing after school.

AMBASSADOR: Why?

STUDENT: Because I thought if you weren't busy, maybe you and I could go get some ice cream.

AMBASSADOR: Actually, I am busy after school.

STUDENT: What are you doing?

AMBASSADOR: Uh, homework.

STUDENT: Maybe we could do our homework together.

AMBASSADOR: Actually, I'm doing it with a tutor.

STUDENT: Oh. Well, how about tomorrow?

AMBASSADOR: I don't think so. I'm busy. Look, I gotta go. I'm late for class.

STUDENT: Can I walk you to class?

AMBASSADOR: Uh, no; I'm really late. See you!

The Ambassador turns to pretend to walk away, and then turns back to the student.

AMBASSADOR: So what just happened?

STUDENT: I asked her out, but she had homework and couldn't go out with me.

AMBASSADOR: Do you think she really had homework?

STUDENT: Yeah, why?

AMBASSADOR: Sometimes when people don't want to do things, they don't give the real reason why. They're just trying to be polite.

STUDENT: But that's lying. That isn't polite.

AMBASSADOR: I know, but they might think you don't know they're lying to you and don't want to hurt your feelings. Which isn't right, but it's better than being mean, in their minds.

Many students with autism miss colloquial expressions and nuances; the student clearly did not understand the brush-off, so he continued to ask away. But he is now upset and feels deceived; it is the Ambassador's job to redirect him toward understanding that people should deal only with others who want to deal with them; the alternative will simply lead to more frustration and confusion.

AMBASSADOR: If a person keeps finding ways to say "no," it means she doesn't want to go out with you. But if she says "no," and then comes back with a different plan, it means she does want to go out with you, okay?

STUDENT: Okay.

AMBASSADOR: Just understand that you'll have to be flexible. The person might want to go out with you but have plans that interfere. If that person tries to ask you out in return, then keep trying to figure out a plan that works for both of you, okay?

STUDENT: Okay.

AMBASSADOR: Great. Let's try that again.

Situation Two:

The Ambassador comes back over to the student, who approaches her.

STUDENT: Hi, (Ambassador's name). What's up?

AMBASSADOR: Not much.

STUDENT: I was wondering what you were doing after school.

AMBASSADOR: Actually, I'm a little busy after school.

STUDENT: What are you doing?

AMBASSADOR: Homework. I have an appointment with my tutor.

STUDENT: Oh.

AMBASSADOR: But actually, what are you doing tomorrow after school?

STUDENT: Actually, tomorrow is okay with me. Do you want to do our homework together?

AMBASSADOR: We could do that. Or we could go to a movie.

STUDENT: But I have homework.

AMBASSADOR: I'd really love to go to a movie.

STUDENT: I know—how about we do our homework first, and then go to a movie?

AMBASSADOR: That sounds great! Thanks so much for asking me out; I think we're going to have a great time hanging out together.

Outro

Asking someone out is one of the toughest things that a student can do, even if that student does not have autism. The Ambassador taught the student how to recognize the difference between someone who genuinely wishes to go out on a date and someone who is subtly rejecting the date proposal. In the case with the successful date proposal, the Ambassador needs to remind the student to be flexible; in the above example, the Ambassador, as the date, did not want to do homework but rather wanted to see a movie. So the student took the Ambassador's advice and worked out a plan that worked for both of them. Like our other module, **Making a Plan,** this module can be used as a starting-off point to teach students with autism how to make other typical social engagements, like going to movies or sporting events, or just hanging out at friends' houses. As with all other modules, it is imperative that Ambassadors anticipate distracting situations that might arise and use their training to refocus the student's attention back on the task at hand.

Cafeteria Etiquette

An Autism Ambassadors
Original Module

Intro

This module instructs Ambassadors how to teach proper cafeteria etiquette to students with autism, which will in turn help them to build tangible social relationships and, ultimately, greater self-esteem.

A typical school day consists of a time to eat, whether it be lunch or recess time. In many cases this time incorporates a variety of conversational tools (refer to our module **Finding Friends at Lunch**). However, eating is an extremely significant part of these breaks from school, and students with autism frequently come across as displaying a disregard for dining etiquette that can be off-putting to even the most seasoned middle and high school lunch hour veterans. As a result, many students with autism find themselves ostracized and/or picked on during lunch or recess hours, which only increases their already considerable anxiety and causes them to feel more isolated than they already do.

The module will simulate a lunch area setting, with desks lined up in rows to represent cafeteria seats, and a tape recorder or CD player present to provide background cafeteria noise (clanking of silverware, etc.). Should an actual cafeteria be available in which to work, Ambassadors should take full advantage of it, as it is always preferable to use as realistic a setting as possible whenever enacting any Autism Ambassador modules.

We will require other students to role-play everything from the student with autism to the other students in the lunch area. The student simulators will sit at seats near the student with autism, while the Ambassador will sit in a seat next to the student with autism.

As with all of our other modules, should the student show signs of extended disengagement or display self-stimulatory behavior with her hands, the Ambassador should refer to our introductory module **Pay Attention/Calm Hands** in order to get the student to be fully present for the lesson.

We are now ready to begin. The Ambassador and the student with autism enter the cafeteria.

AMBASSADOR: Oh look—there's (name of student with whom both the Ambassador and student with autism are familiar). Let's go sit with him.

The Ambassador and student with autism sit down with the other students at the lunch table and greetings are exchanged.

> As stated in the Intro, please refer to our module **Finding Friends at Lunch** to address the social anxiety–related issues pertaining to students with autism in cafeterias and other public settings.

STUDENT: [grabs a piece of chicken from her lunch and begins to eat, ripping the flesh apart with her fingers]

The other students look on, trying not to appear too grossed out, but they can barely disguise their disgust.

AMBASSADOR: (Student's name), would you like to use a fork and a knife? I think it would make it easier for you to eat.

> The Ambassador should anticipate the improper eating habits of the student with autism and should be prepared with napkins, plastic silverware, or even a bib if need be.

STUDENT: [ignores the Ambassador, continues to eat while the Ambassador takes out two sets of forks and knives and carves his own food up with one set while handing the other set to the student with autism]

AMBASSADOR: Here, I have an extra fork and knife. You can have the ones I'm not using.

> The Ambassador should not correct the student harshly but rather should play down the student's eating habits and instead lead by example. As with all of our modules, Ambassadors need to remember that they are role models for students with autism, who will likely copy the socially acceptable behavior of the Ambassador when correctly prompted to do so.

The Ambassador hands the fork and knife to the student, who stares blankly, holding them.

AMBASSADOR: It looks like you're having a hard time with the fork and knife. Here, let me help you.

The Ambassador gently takes the fork and knife and uses them to help the student with autism slice up the chicken.

Many students with autism have significant tactile issues. Ambassadors should always be sensitive to this and be gentle whenever any physical activity is involved. (Refer to our module **Playing Football** and both the modules in our **Field Trip** series for further notes on this subject.)

STUDENT: [begins to eat with a fork and a knife, but chews with mouth open]

AMBASSADOR: So, who here saw (name of movie) this weekend?

Movies are always a good conversational ice breaker, but please reference our other module, **Finding Favorite Movies,** to learn further tips about discussing pop cultural references with students with autism. As is always the case, should the student with autism be unfamiliar with the Ambassador's movie reference, the Ambassador should continue to refer to other movies until he finds one with which the student with autism is familiar.

STUDENT: [with mouth full of food] I did! It was really cool.

AMBASSADOR: (Student's name), I'm really interested to hear what you thought about the movie. But can you wait until after you're done chewing?

STUDENT: Why?

AMBASSADOR: Because you wouldn't want that food falling out of your mouth, right? If it falls on the floor, it will get dirty and that will mean you won't get to enjoy it.

Even if the reason the Ambassador is giving is technically false, sometimes a more pragmatic or utilitarian reason will be easier for students with autism to understand than a more abstract explanation like it's rude to chew with your mouth open and talk with your mouth full of food.

STUDENT: [begins to chew properly]

AMBASSADOR: Good chewing with your mouth closed!

> As with all our other modules, Ambassadors should always go out of their way to reinforce proper behavior, no matter how seemingly mundane it might be.

AMBASSADOR: See how I'm talking without food in my mouth? Then when I want to eat, I chew my food with my mouth closed, but I don't talk. Like this. [demonstrates, and then swallows his food] Now that I'm done chewing and swallowing my food, I can talk about anything I want. And so can you!

Another student stands up and exits the lunch area, leaving behind her tray filled with half-eaten food morsels. The student with autism leans over to take some food, but is stopped by the Ambassador.

AMBASSADOR: (Student's name), we don't eat from other trays.

STUDENT: Why not?

AMBASSADOR: For the same reasons we don't take food from another person's mouth. Because we don't want to share germs and get sick.

STUDENT: [leaves the food on the other tray alone]

AMBASSADOR: Great table manners!

Outro

This module covers essential eating habits and table manners during lunchtime, such as the proper use of utensils and the appropriate way to chew and talk. The basic principles of the module—pointing out inappropriate eating habits, giving reasons why they shouldn't be used, and demonstrating proper etiquette—can be applied to any unhygienic or unacceptable cafeteria behavior. By teaching the student with autism more socially acceptable eating habits, the Ambassador is empowering the student to be able to navigate the lunch room area and its social etiquette with confidence, which in turn builds better self-esteem.

As with all other modules, it is imperative that Ambassadors anticipate distracting situations that might arise and use their training to refocus the student's attention back on the task at hand. If necessary, it is fine for the Ambassador to improvise, as long as the improvisation falls well within the range of acceptable behavior. Should more assistance be necessary, the Ambassador should not hesitate to engage a teacher or schoolyard supervisor.

Cursing and Offensive Language

An Autism Ambassadors Original Module

Intro

The purpose of this module is to teach students with autism how to make productive contributions to social and academic environments by refraining from using curse words and language that other students might find offensive for a variety of reasons.

Middle and high school students (especially the former) are at a point in their development where they find themselves frequently pushing the envelope of what is considered to be socially acceptable behavior. Although many students have decent values and, when they are asked objectively and are given the opportunity to behave independently, disdain poor behavior, they nonetheless often find themselves following peer pressure and acting rudely or disrespectfully (or worse) to their fellow students. Students with autism, most of whom do not have natural filters and therefore might lack inherent empathy, can be especially susceptible to bad behavior and might act in a manner far worse than that of their peers. Thus it is important to teach them the ramifications of curse words and offensive language.

This module takes place in a lunch room in school; to replicate a lunch room setting, we need other students, which we will select from among the students in Ambassador training. All Ambassador trainees role-play and take turns being the student who needs assistance as well as other members of the class milling about.

As with all of our other modules, should the student show signs of extended disengagement or display self-stimulatory behavior with his hands, the Ambassador should refer to our introductory module **Pay Attention/Calm Hands** in order to get the student to be fully present for the lesson.

We are now ready to begin. The Ambassador leads the student with autism over to a lunch table and they sit down.

AMBASSADOR: (Student's name), today we are going to discuss words that hurt people's feelings.

STUDENT: [looks around; acts uninterested]

AMBASSADOR: The reason we are going to discuss these words is because sometimes people say them and other people laugh, but it really isn't funny.

STUDENT: Then why do they laugh?

AMBASSADOR: That's a really good question! Why do you think they laugh?

STUDENT: Because it's funny?

AMBASSADOR: That's usually why people laugh, but with bad language there's often a different reason why they laugh. Sometimes it's because they're uncomfortable and they don't know how else to act. Do you ever get uncomfortable?

STUDENT: Yes.

> While it is a good idea to ask this question—the more the Ambassador can engage the student to explore his own feelings, the more likely the module will have a successful outcome—the student might not feel comfortable enough to answer this question, so the Ambassador needs to be ready to move to the next step, as outlined below.

AMBASSADOR: Sometimes I get uncomfortable and I start to sweat. Or I start to hum. Do you ever do things like that when you're uncomfortable?

STUDENT: [nods]

AMBASSADOR: That's what I mean. People do all kinds of things when they are uncomfortable. And one of those things is laugh. And people laugh sometimes when other people say mean things that make them uncomfortable.

STUDENT: [hums, clucks tongue]

AMBASSADOR: Have you ever heard people say mean things about people with autism?

STUDENT: I like trains.

> Once again, the student might feel too uncomfortable to answer the question directly, so he might substitute an answer that reflects a point of comfort. This is a delicate topic for Ambassadors, who must redirect the student back to the subject at hand without invalidating the student, who might be feeling much more than he is letting on.

AMBASSADOR: I like train,s too, but right now I'd really like to know if you've ever heard people say mean things about people with autism.

STUDENT: Yes.

AMBASSADOR: Like what kinds of mean things have you heard people say about people with autism?

STUDENT: People say that people with autism are freaks.

AMBASSADOR: How did it make you feel?

STUDENT: Sad.

AMBASSADOR: And it didn't make you want to laugh, right?

STUDENT: No.

AMBASSADOR: Because people with autism are not freaks. They have a disability. Can you think of other people who have a disability?

STUDENT: People in wheelchairs.

AMBASSADOR: Right. So people with a disability can be made to feel sad when other people say mean things about their disability. But you don't have to have a disability for someone to say something that makes you feel sad. Did you know that?

STUDENT: Yes.

AMBASSADOR: Good. I never want to make anyone else feel sad because of something I say. Do you feel that way, too?

STUDENT: Yes.

Some students with autism lack basic empathy, so they will need incentives and disincentives in order to refrain from saying hurtful or offensive things. Although Ambassadors are not in a position to take away toys or privileges, they can explore other motivational tools, like emphasizing that the student will not be listened to by the teacher, or will have to sit elsewhere during lunch, et cetera. Ambassadors should know the student's habits in order to factor them into this step of the module.

AMBASSADOR: I'm happy to hear that. Let's talk about some language that might hurt other people's feelings. Can you think of any words that might hurt other people's feelings?

STUDENT: Stupid. Weirdo.

AMBASSADOR: Those are definitely some hurtful words. Good for you for pointing them out to me. I think it's safe to say that any word that would make you feel sad would make someone else feel sad. Can you think of any other words that are just wrong to say?

STUDENT: [flaps hands]

As the module gets into more colorful language, the student might react in an increasingly anxious manner, especially if the student is sensitive to noise or sounds. Ambassadors should anticipate this and be prepared to switch to writing down the words if necessary.

AMBASSADOR: There are a lot of words that we shouldn't say, ever. Not in school, not at home, not to other people when we're out with them, because they make us look bad AND hurt other people's feelings. [Ambassador writes out a number of curse words on a sheet of paper.]

Ambassadors should always be aware of school decorum and keep the volume of both their voices and their student partners' voices to a minimum.

STUDENT: I hear those words a lot.

AMBASSADOR: Me, too. Where do you hear them?

STUDENT: Movies. Music.

AMBASSADOR: Sometimes our favorite movie actors and singers use bad language. But that's make believe. Real people shouldn't use that language.

STUDENTS: Other kids do.

AMBASSADOR: Yes, but remember what we said about bad and hurtful language, and how sometimes other kids use it because they're not comfortable? Let's not be like them, okay?

STUDENT: Okay.

Outro

The Ambassador was taught first to identify the dynamics behind hurtful and inappropriate language and then to help the student identify the language itself and why he shouldn't use it. Additionally, we pointed to instances in the media where bad language is used and addressed the challenges involved in teaching students with autism how to be discerning in these instances.

As with all other modules, it is imperative that Ambassadors anticipate distracting situations that might arise and use their training to refocus the student's attention back on the task at hand. If necessary, it is fine for the Ambassador to improvise, as long as the improvisation falls well within the range of acceptable behavior. Should more assistance be necessary, the Ambassador should not hesitate to engage a teacher or schoolyard supervisor.

Explaining Your Diagnosis to Friends

An Autism Ambassadors Original Module

Intro

The purpose of this module is to teach students how to let their peers know about their autism and, in doing so, create a better social and academic environment not only for themselves but for their peers as well.

Any time a person has a disability, whether it is autism or anything else, it is in her best interest to own it rather than keeping it a secret. Whenever people are forthcoming about something that makes them different, they tend to be surprised not only by how well people can relate on some universal level but also by how much kindness will come their way on account of their directness.

This module takes place in a lunch room in school; to replicate a lunch room setting, we need other students, which we will select from among the students in Ambassador training. All Ambassador trainees role-play and take turns being the student who needs assistance as well as other members of the class milling about.

As with all of our other modules, should the student with autism show signs of extended disengagement or display self-stimulatory behavior with her hands, the Ambassador should refer to our introductory module **Pay Attention/Calm Hands** in order to get the student to be fully present for the lesson.

We are now ready to begin. The Ambassador leads the student with autism over to a group of students and they sit down.

AMBASSADOR: Hi everyone, my name is (Ambassador's name). This is (student's name).

STUDENTS: Hi (student's name)!

AMBASSADOR: Before we sit down, I want to let you all know something. I'm deaf in my left ear, so in order for me to hear you fully, you need to talk into my right ear.

> The Ambassador should take the lead and model the situation using his own disability as an example—anything from wearing glasses to ADHD to even something as seemingly mundane as acne, anything to increase the comfort level of those around him. Chances are the Ambassador will not have a clinical diagnosis, and if he does not know someone well who has one to ask to join this exercise to help set an example, he can use the deaf ear example or any deficiency he feels is appropriate for the purposes of this module.

STUDENT AT TABLE: I am so sorry to hear that—how long has that been the case?

AMBASSADOR: Since I was born. It's okay; I just wanted to let you know so you didn't think I was weird or that I was ignoring you when you're talking; sometimes I just can't hear what people are saying.

> It is important that the Ambassador explain exactly both the nature of the disability and any considerations the students should make on his behalf. Levity is the key, but humor should be avoided so the disclosure of the disability is not misinterpreted as sarcasm or being flip.

AMBASSADOR: I also try to get places early so I can choose a seat that enables me to point my good ear toward whatever I need to hear.

STUDENT AT TABLE: Well, we will make sure to try to speak into your good ear when we talk to you, and if you ever need anything repeated, please just let us know. And if any of us forgets, please make sure to remind us, okay?

AMBASSADOR: Okay, I will. Thanks.

The Ambassador turns to the student with autism.

AMBASSADOR: (Student's name), do you want to share something with the group like the problem I just shared?

STUDENT: I don't like cafeteria food.

> Should the student with autism not respond to the prompt, the Ambassador should continue to lead her there, saying things like, "Do you have something about you that requires some extra help or understanding sometimes?"

AMBASSADOR:	You know what? I don't like cafeteria food either. And neither does anyone else, really. And I think everyone has that problem, just like everyone has other problems or disabilities. Because everyone has something that causes some difficulty. It's nothing to be ashamed about, right?
OTHER STUDENTS:	Right.

> Depending on the comfort level of the student with autism, it might be helpful for other students to share their problems: fear of flying, allergy to bee stings, et cetera.

STUDENT:	I have autism.
AMBASSADOR:	Oh, I didn't know that! What can we do to help you? How can we work with you so we can understand what you need?
STUDENT:	[fidgets]

> Some higher functioning students might be able to answer this question immediately; they might find the admission on the part of the Ambassador (and, if necessary, the other students at the table) liberating.

AMBASSADOR:	Do you sometimes have a hard time paying attention?
STUDENT:	Yes.
AMBASSADOR:	So do we need to understand that about you and not be upset if we don't think you're paying attention? Just like people shouldn't be upset with me if I can't hear them?
STUDENT:	Yes—I would really like it if you did that.
AMBASSADOR:	Great! Thanks for explaining that to us! That's really helpful! What other things will help us understand you better?
STUDENT:	I like trains.

> Students with autism will frequently perseverate, or focus single-mindedly on a subject of their fascination at the expense of another. They also frequently pepper their conversations with a high number of non sequiturs. The above is an example of both: While the student might, in her mind, be answering the question posed by the Ambassador, the student might also be veering away from the topic of the challenges posed by autism, so the Ambassador needs to be ready to steer the student back on to the topic at hand.

AMBASSADOR: That's wonderful. Maybe we can talk about trains later, but I'd love to hear more about what we can do to understand more about autism.

STUDENT: Sometimes my mother tells me I don't make sense.

AMBASSADOR: Does that mean you have a hard time talking about the same things other people are talking about?

STUDENT: Yes.

AMBASSADOR: Well, that's okay. Since we're talking about autism right now, anything you want to share about autism would be really good for us to know. And later on we can talk about anything else you'd like, okay?

STUDENT: Okay.

Outro

The objective of this module was to familiarize and desensitize typical students to the issues faced by students with autism. For this module, we taught the Ambassador first how to introduce his own disability and then to help integrate the student with autism into the group by prompting the student to address her own diagnosis. It should be noted that the prompts we outlined above should serve as merely the beginning of a longer conversation about the student's special needs (her tactile issues, anxieties, fears, etc.). Understanding a student with autism is a complicated process, but one for which a well-trained, empathetic Ambassador can provide a great deal of assistance.

As with all other modules, it is imperative that Ambassadors anticipate distracting situations that might arise and use their training to refocus the student's attention back on the task at hand. If necessary, it is fine for the Ambassador to improvise, as long as the improvisation falls well within the range of acceptable behavior. Should more assistance be necessary, the Ambassador should not hesitate to engage a teacher or schoolyard supervisor.

Finding Friends at Lunch

An Autism Ambassadors
Original Module

Intro

The purpose of this module is to teach students with autism how to successfully navigate the lunchroom or cafeteria to find and sit with friends, which can be a daunting task for typical students but is especially so for students with autism.

Lunchtime is a welcome and necessary respite from class activities that every student needs and should look forward to, but lunch areas often involve chaotic social hierarchies that can be disorienting for students with autism. Sitting and eating alone can frequently bring unwanted attention from other, sometimes less sympathetic students, which in turn can cause students with autism to withdraw even further from their surroundings. The goal is to get students with autism to be able to integrate themselves into their surroundings so they feel like they fit in and can enjoy the lunchtime break.

The module will simulate a lunch area setting, with desks lined up in rows to represent cafeteria seats, and a tape recorder or CD player present to provide background noise (clanking of silverware, etc.). We will require other students to role-play everything from the student with special needs to the other students in the lunch area. The student simulators will sit at seats near the student with autism, while the Ambassador will sit in a seat next to the student with autism.

As with all of our other modules, should the student show signs of extended disengagement or display self-stimulatory behavior with his hands, the Ambassador should refer to our introductory module **Pay Attention/Calm Hands** in order to get the student to be fully present for the lesson.

We are now ready to begin. The Ambassador leads the student with autism into the lunch area. Both hold trays.

AMBASSADOR: (Student's name), it's lunchtime. Where do you think would be a good place for us to sit?

STUDENT: [looks around the room; has no idea what to do next]

AMBASSADOR: Hmm, let's look around the room. I see a lot of people sitting with their friends. Why do you think people like to sit with other people during lunch?

STUDENT: [looks down at tray and darts eyes around, mumbling nervously]

AMBASSADOR: I think it would be a good idea to sit with someone. That way we can have a conversation while we eat. That's much more interesting and fun than just eating alone and not doing anything social.

> Students with autism frequently are not as motivated to make social connections as are their peers. Thus it is important to explain to them why they should add a social component to an otherwise utilitarian task such as eating lunch.

AMBASSADOR: Who do you want to eat with? Who's really nice?

STUDENT: [looks around; points at an empty table]

> Given any task involving social interaction, the student might feel tremendous anxiety and might try to figure a way out of the situation. Pointing to the empty table is a way for the student to feel safe, since an empty table offers no social challenges that the student might find daunting. The Ambassador needs to anticipate any kind of evasive action on the part of the student and keep him on task.

AMBASSADOR: I like that table, too, and think it would be a nice place to sit if I needed to be by myself to read something, but right now I think we should find a table full of people we like so we can sit with them. Do you see any students you like who we can sit with?

STUDENT: [looks around, spots a student and points to her]

AMBASSADOR: I agree—(other student's name) is really nice. Do you want to go sit over at that table with (other student's name)?

STUDENT: [starts to shake his lunch tray back and forth]

AMBASSADOR: It's okay—since (other student's name) is so nice, I'll bet (other student's) friends are really nice, too.

Even though the student with autism might know and feel positively about the student with whom he is going to sit, the student with autism might not be familiar with the other students at the table. In general, it is important to emphasize associative logic—that kid is nice, and people who are nice tend to sit with other nice people—as much as possible when it comes to students with autism; little, if anything, should be taken for granted when it comes to explaining social behavior.

The student starts to follow the Ambassador across the lunch area to the table where the other students are sitting. We hear a loud CRASH of dishes from the CD player/tape recorder.

STUDENT: [puts his tray down and covers his ears, makes nervous noises]

AMBASSADOR: Oh, that's just some dishes that fell. That happens all the time. It's nothing to worry about.

Students with autism are frequently sensitive to loud noises and background disruptions; it is important for the Ambassador to factor the noise or actions into the dialogue and make the noises as familiar and unthreatening as possible.

The Ambassador and student sit down at the other table.

Outro

The objective of this module was to guide students through the disorienting, frightening environment of the lunch area and help the student find a friend while desensitizing the student with autism to external noises. For this module, we taught Ambassadors how to incorporate outside distractions into the dialogue to ease anxiety. Once the student has become acclimated to finding friends and has generalized the process of navigating the lunch area, the Ambassador should work with him on other lunchroom-related skills (see module **Eating Habits**).

As with all other modules, it is imperative that Ambassadors anticipate distracting situations that might arise and use their training to refocus the student's attention back on the task at hand. If necessary, it is fine for the Ambassador to improvise, as long as the improvisation falls well within the range of acceptable behavior. Should more assistance be necessary, the Ambassador should not hesitate to engage a teacher or school supervisor.

Finding Favorite Popular Music

An Autism Ambassadors Original Module

Intro

The purpose of this module is to teach students how to identify popular music for casual conversational purposes and, should those students be musically inclined, for their own musical listening pleasure as well. Additionally, since the technological aspect of finding popular songs is so important, we will address how to find the actual songs via programs like iTunes and Spotify.

Because popular music is such a staple of middle school and high school students' conversation, it is an excellent way for students with autism to blend in with their peers in the lunch areas and anywhere else their peers gather. Additionally, the prevalence of popular music in everything from video games (Guitar Hero) and television shows (*American Idol, X Factor*) offers even more opportunities for the student with autism to learn about, and process the information from, this medium.

This module takes place in the lunch area in school. To replicate a lunch area setting, we need other students, who, during Ambassador training, role-play and take turns being the student with autism. The student simulators will sit at desks near the student with autism while another student will sit next to the student with autism and perform the duties of the Ambassador. Because we will be working in a format that requires a fair amount of technological access, the Ambassador should have either a laptop or desktop computer (Apple products are especially useful given that we will be discussing iTunes) with Internet access handy.

As with all of our other modules, should the student show signs of extended disengagement or display self-stimulatory behavior with her hands, the Ambassador should refer to our introductory module **Pay Attention/Calm Hands** in order to get the student to be fully present for the lesson.

We are now ready to begin.

AMBASSADOR: (Student's name), let's have a talk about music. I love music. Do you?

STUDENT: [sits down, starts playing with hands]

AMBASSADOR: I love music. Do you?

STUDENT: [stares at hands, looks off to the side]

> This situation is unlike the situation with the prompt below, where the Ambassador must keep trying different artist names until the Ambassador finds one the student knows. In this situation, it is not crucial for the Ambassador to get a response to this prompt. Most students, both typical and those with special needs, like music and, accordingly, the prompt can be viewed as a rhetorical question, a casual way to open the conversation and engage the student. Should the student not answer "yes," the Ambassador should feel free to move on to the question that follows the response below.

STUDENT: Yes.

AMBASSADOR: Great answering! What kind of music do you like?

STUDENT: [ignores Ambassador, stares off to the side]

AMBASSADOR: What kind of music do you like? I like (artist's name).

> If the student ignores the Ambassador, the Ambassador should repeat the question, making a point to add a name or song to prompt the student. Also, the Ambassador should start with an obvious Top 40 artist, but should not assume that the student is familiar with that artist; the Ambassador should keep naming names of artists until he comes across one with whom the student is familiar and wishes to discuss.

STUDENT: I like (artist's name), too.

AMBASSADOR: Great! That's something we can talk about together! What's your favorite song of his?

STUDENT: [stares off into space, starts humming]

> Should the student start to hum one of the artist's songs, the Ambassador should be prepared to use this as a conversational prompt. If the song is by another artist, the Ambassador should use that as a prompt to discuss the other artist's work.

AMBASSADOR: My favorite song is (name of song). What's your favorite song?

STUDENT: (Name of song)

> This situation is similar to the one outlined above, where the Ambassador kept trying different artist names until the Ambassador found one with the student recognized. Should the student not name any songs, the Ambassador should be prepared to name songs until he comes across one with which the student is familiar and wishes to discuss.

AMBASSADOR: I like that song, too!

> This pattern of interaction can be used for the music-related TV shows as well. (For example, Who is your favorite contestant on *American Idol?* What was your favorite song of hers?

AMBASSADOR: I like to download music on iTunes. Do you have iTunes?

STUDENT: No.

AMBASSADOR: Do you have Spotify?

STUDENT: No.

> Should the student say yes to either question, the Ambassador should ask if the student knows how it works, and then move to a demonstration. Spotify is potentially an easier program from which to work, as it is immediately downloadable.

AMBASSADOR: Here, it's really easy to use. First you download the program. [downloads and installs the program] Next, you set up a playlist. Let's call ours "(Student's name)'s Tunes." [sets up a playlist folder] Then you go look for songs in the search window, find them, and drag them over to the folder. Let's start with (song they discussed).

The Ambassador demonstrates, and then hands the laptop (or desktop mouse) over to the student.

AMBASSADOR: Your turn!

The student builds a playlist, using either iTunes or Spotify.

AMBASSADOR: You know what? I think I'm going to listen to that playlist on the way home from school today. Great idea!

Outro

For this module, we started by having the Ambassador identify a popular music artist that he could discuss with the student with autism. The conversation then segued into song titles and gave the student with autism an opportunity to discuss her favorites. Ambassadors should make a point to extend the conversation for as long as possible, which will build the confidence of the student with autism not only for this topic, but for all other pop culture–related topics (sports, fashion) as well. Finally, the Ambassador taught the student how to use programs like iTunes and Spotify, so the student could build her own playlists. Note that this module can and should be used in conjunction with other socially oriented modules, such as **Finding Friends, Explaining Your Diagnosis,** et cetera.

As with all other modules, it is imperative that Ambassadors anticipate distracting situations that might arise and use their training to refocus the student's attention back on the task at hand. If necessary, it is fine for the Ambassador to improvise, as long as the improvisation falls well within the range of acceptable behavior. Should more assistance be necessary, the Ambassador should not hesitate to engage a teacher or school supervisor.

Joining a Club at School

An Autism Ambassadors Original Module

Intro

The purpose of this module is to get students to learn how to join one, or ultimately several, of the extracurricular club options that schools offer and that might provide the student with autism with not only a social outlet but also a place of focus for his outside interests.

Club membership is viewed by students as a badge of belonging. Clubs are organizations in which students can meet and mingle with other like-minded students. Students with autism, however, frequently have difficulty determining what clubs to belong to and, should they figure that out, how to fit in once they are there. Their anxiety frequently prevents them from taking those all-important first steps: identifying clubs that might be compatible with their interests and then taking action in order to join those clubs.

This module takes place in the classroom in school; to replicate a club room setting, we need other students, which we will select from among the students in Ambassador training. All Ambassador trainees role-play and take turns being the student who needs assistance as well as other members of the club milling about and performing their club-related duties.

As with all of our other modules, should the student show signs of extended disengagement or display self-stimulatory behavior with his hands, the Ambassador should refer to our introductory module **Pay Attention/Calm Hands** in order to get the student to be fully present for the lesson.

We are now ready to begin. The Ambassador leads the student with autism over to the door of the club room and pauses.

AMBASSADOR: (Student's name), now that school is over, a lot of students are going to their afterschool clubs. There are so many to choose from. I'm in (names one of the clubs to which she belongs). Have you heard of it?

STUDENT: [stares at something off in the distance]

AMBASSADOR: [repeating the question] Have you heard of (name of club)?

STUDENT: No.

> Whether or not the Ambassador thinks the student has heard of the club, the Ambassador should describe it, as detailed below. Students with autism frequently have terrible anxiety when it comes to social activities, and the student might be doing whatever he can to find an easy way out of the conversation. Ambassadors should never permit the student to disengage but rather should continue to illustrate what makes clubs worth being a part of and the people who belong to them worth knowing.

AMBASSADOR: What I love about my club is that it gives me a chance to participate in something at school that isn't about studying. And the kids are really nice, because they like the same things I like.

> As they do in other modules, Ambassadors should take every opportunity to use themselves as examples for the student with autism, even if they do not think there is an inherent compatibility.

AMBASSADOR: Do you think you would like to join a club?

STUDENT: [flaps hands; looks nervous]

AMBASSADOR: You don't have to join one, but it'll be really fun if you do. You can pick something that you like to do, and everyone in the club will also like to do it. What are some of the things you like to do?

> It is important to both emphasize and address the element of choice involved in joining a club. For starters, if a student feels that joining a club is required, his anxiety will rise, which is why it is important to begin by explaining that club membership is not mandatory. The Ambassador should, however, also be aware that too many choices can also increase anxiety, which is why the Ambassador needs to hone in immediately on the specific interests of the student with autism.

STUDENT: I like trains.

> As we have discussed in other modules, students with autism frequently exhibit single-minded attention to their interests. Should the student answer the Ambassador's question with a subject for which there is no club, the Ambassador should be ready to steer the student back to the clubs that do exist.

AMBASSADOR: I like trains, but I don't know if they have a club for them here.

STUDENT: Yes they do.

AMBASSADOR: Okay, maybe I'm wrong; let's check the club lists.

Schools have different clubs available, and the Ambassador should have at least a basic working knowledge of not only all the clubs available, but their schedules as well. Should the choices be too numerous for the Ambassador to remember, she should obtain or download a copy of clubs and their schedules.

AMBASSADOR: Do you see a club for kids who like trains?

STUDENT: No.

AMBASSADOR: Me neither. Let's look down the list and see if we can find a club you might like.

STUDENT: [scans the list]

AMBASSADOR: Do you like movies?

STUDENT: Yes.

AMBASSADOR: I like movies, too! And there's a club for kids who like movies that meets after school every (day of the week the club meets). Let's go join!

The Ambassador leads the student into the club room.

AMBASSADOR: Hey, everyone, this is (student's name). He is interested in joining your movie club.

Ambassadors need to be sensitive to the potential challenges involved in introducing a student with autism to a new group of people. Please refer to our module **Explaining Your Diagnosis** for further assistance in this area.

CLUB MEMBERS: Hi, (student name).

AMBASSADOR: Maybe you guys can explain what your club does so that he can make a decision.

CLUB MEMBER: We talk about movies, screen movies in class sometimes, arrange for guest speakers who work in the movie business to talk to us over Skype, and sometimes we arrange for our club to go to the movies on weekends.

AMBASSADOR: (Student's name), does that sound good to you?

STUDENT: Yes.

Even though the student says yes, he will likely be overwhelmed and might require more from the Ambassador to truly understand what is involved in joining a club. A good way to start is for the Ambassador to issue a prompt, as illustrated below.

AMBASSADOR: What are you guys doing right now?

CLUB MEMBER: We're discussing (movie title).

AMBASSADOR: (Student's name), have you ever seen that movie?

STUDENT: Yes—I love that movie.

Should the film be unfamiliar to the student with autism, the Ambassador should try to steer the conversation to a movie the Ambassador knows the student has seen; at the very least, the Ambassador should encourage the student to sit and listen to the discussion.

Outro

The objective of this module was to desensitize students with autism to the considerable challenges of participating in extracurricular school clubs and activities. For this module, we taught the Ambassador first how to introduce the idea of afterschool clubs, and then to help integrate the student with autism into the club once he had joined.

As with all other modules, it is imperative that Ambassadors anticipate distracting situations that might arise and use their training to refocus the student's attention back on the task at hand, always making a point to establish a comfort level for the student.

Making a Plan

An Autism Ambassadors
Original Module

Intro

This module is called **Making a Plan**. The objective of this module is to teach students with autism to initiate social plans and react appropriately when asked to engage in a social plan.

Asking peers to hang out or go somewhere can be daunting for typical students, let alone students with autism. Teaching students with autism appropriate responses and questions involves a great deal of planning and anticipation. Note that in this module, unlike other modules, we will cover two situations: In one, the student with autism asks the Ambassador to hang out, and in the other, the Ambassador asks the student with autism the same.

This module takes place in a hallway setting in school; to replicate a hallway setting, we need other students, which we will select from among the students in Ambassador training. All Ambassador trainees role-play and take turns being the student who needs assistance as well as other members of the class milling about.

As with all of our other modules, should the student show signs of extended disengagement or display self-stimulatory behavior with her hands, the Ambassador should refer to our introductory module **Pay Attention/Calm Hands** in order to get the student to be fully present for the lesson.

We are now ready to begin.

Situation One:

AMBASSADOR: Hi, (student's name). What's up?

STUDENT: [looking down] Not much.

AMBASSADOR: What are you doing during lunch?

STUDENT: Eating lunch.

> Many students with autism miss colloquial expressions or nuances; the student above interprets the Ambassador's question literally as opposed to understanding that the Ambassador was asking her if she wanted to have a social plan during lunch.

AMBASSADOR: Oh, I'm going to be eating lunch, too. Are you eating lunch with anyone today?

STUDENT: [shakes her head]

AMBASSADOR: Cool. Do you want to hang out during lunch and eat together?

> It is a good idea, since we are using the colloquial expression *hang out,* to combine it with the more utilitarian expression *eat together* just in case the student with autism does not know what *hang out* means.

STUDENT: I like trains.

AMBASSADOR: I like trains, too. Maybe we can talk about that during lunch.

> Students with autism frequently have a difficult time staying focused on one subject, especially when their anxiety manifests, as it often will whenever social issues are at hand. Ambassadors should aim to gently steer them back on topic and keep them focused.

STUDENT: [plays with hands, stares off to the side]

AMBASSADOR: So will I see you during lunch?

STUDENT: Maybe.

> There are many reasons that students with autism might not want to hang out, including insecurity, apathy, and lack of social skills. Ambassadors should not be daunted but rather should be unyielding in their enthusiasm and positive energy.

AMBASSADOR: We're in the same period, so we can sit together. I'd really like that. I'm sure we'll have a great time together; we can talk about anything you want. Would you like to sit together during lunch?

STUDENT: Okay.

AMBASSADOR: Great! It will be really fun to hang out. See you in the lunch area?

STUDENT: Okay, see you there.

Situation Two:

AMBASSADOR: Hi, (student's name).

STUDENT: Hi.

AMBASSADOR: What are you doing during lunch?

While stopping short of actually asking the student with autism to hang out, the Ambassador should guide the student in the right direction so that the student can see that a social plan is in the making. Should the student not get the hint, or choose to disengage, the Ambassador should continue to lead the student with phrases like "I love sitting with friends and talking during lunch" or "I was hoping to sit with a friend during lunch." Refer to our module **Finding Friends at Lunch** for further help on this subject.

STUDENT: I'm going to come to dinner tonight! It will be a gift for you.

AMBASSADOR: That's great! I definitely want to hang out with you, and I really appreciate your offer of giving me a gift, but I don't think my parents will let me have anyone over for dinner in the next few weeks because I have too much homework. Maybe we can sit together during lunch either today or tomorrow instead?

In the event that the student's response is awkward or inappropriate, as is frequently the case, the Ambassador should try to redirect the student back to the subject at hand.

STUDENT: Okay. Do you like trains? I went on a train once, from my house to downtown.

AMBASSADOR: That's terrific! I went on a train once too, from my house to downtown. It was really fun. You know what else was really fun? Hanging out at lunch with my friends. So are we going to sit together during lunch tomorrow and have fun hanging out?

Any time the student with autism tries to change the subject, the Ambassador should reroute the conversation back to making plans while never ignoring the focus of the student's conversation (i.e., trains). Note that the Ambassador need not worry about a graceful segue from the student's preferred topic back to the task at hand; a simple upbeat acknowledgment of the student's interest, followed by the redirection, is perfectly acceptable.

STUDENT: Yes. So then we can talk about trains?

AMBASSADOR: Yes. But we'll have to eat lunch first. Is that okay with you if we eat lunch together and talk about trains while we do?

The Ambassador should always make sure the student is aware of the plan that they are making together by repeating what the plan is at numerous points in the conversation, as outlined above.

STUDENT: Yes, that's okay with me.

AMBASSADOR: Great! Thanks so much for asking me to lunch; I really appreciate it, and I think we're going to have a great time hanging out together.

Outro

Making a plan is one of the most important skills that a student can learn, whether it be during class or out of school. This module helps the student with autism learn how to both accept and initiate social plans with typical students. It also teaches Ambassadors how to ensure that students with autism are aware of the ramifications and obligations of making a social plan. Ambassadors should use the above module as a starting-off point to teach students with autism how to make other typical social engagements, like going to movies, sporting events, or just hanging out at friends' houses.

As with all other modules, it is imperative that Ambassadors anticipate distracting situations that might arise and use their training to refocus the student's attention back on the task at hand.

School Dance

*An Autism Ambassadors
Original Module*

Intro

The goal of this module is to enable a student with autism to be able to attend a school dance without becoming scared, alarmed, or disoriented. School dances are typically loud, chaotic environments that are filled with blasting music, blinding strobe lights, and students who are both dancing and running around. To a student with autism, this is a veritable perfect storm of disorientation, yet these dances are frequently social highlights that students feel compelled to attend in order to feel like they fit in. For a student with autism to do so, he must go through extensive desensitization, step-by-step, in order to feel comfortable in an environment that, inherently speaking, is anything but.

It is also important to note that some students with autism are just like some typical students in that they have no interest in attending school dances; prior to enacting the exercise, the Ambassador needs to determine if this might be the case with the particular student for whom the module is tailored.

This module takes place in the gym at school, where we will first run desensitization exercises with sound, then simulate the light show part of the dance, and finally add the noise to the light show to recreate as accurate a school dance scenario as possible. To fully replicate a school dance setting, we will also need other students, which we will select from among the students in Ambassador training. All Ambassador trainees role-play and take turns being the student with autism.

You will also need something with which to play loud music (as well as the loud music, preferably contemporary and conducive to being played as loud as possible), as well as a microphone for the Ambassador when it comes time to pretend to be the deejay. A strobe light, or electronic light bank capable of simulating a school dance light show, is less necessary but extremely useful should one be handy.

This module can be used in conjunction with our other modules, **Fire/ Emergency Drill** and **Finding Favorite Popular Music,** both of which cover related subjects.

As with all of our other modules, should the student show signs of extended disengagement or display self-stimulatory behavior with his hands, the Ambassador should refer to our introductory module **Pay Attention/Calm Hands** in order to get the student to be fully present for the lesson.

We are now ready to begin. The student and Ambassador walk into the gym.

AMBASSADOR: (Student's name), do you like to dance?

STUDENT: Yes.

AMBASSADOR: I like to dance, too. This Saturday, there's going to be a big dance at school. Do you want to go to the dance?

STUDENT: Yes.

> As stated in the Intro, the Ambassador needs to make sure that the answer to this question will always be yes.

AMBASSADOR: Great. Me, too. But you know something? I've been in this gym a hundred times, but never when it's completely dark. Do you mind if we turn off the lights for a second?

STUDENT: [shakes his head]

The Ambassador walks over to the light switch and turns it off. Then back on. Then off, on, off, on until it resembles a strobe light.

> Should this step be too difficult for the student to bear, the Ambassador should let the student play with the lights first so he feels more in control.

AMBASSADOR: You know what? That was fun. The gym isn't such a nice-looking place, but it looks pretty cool with the lights going on and off like that. Now for something even more fun: Let's practice our dance steps.

STUDENT: Okay.

> Should the student be unreceptive to this, the Ambassador should just play some music and start dancing with or without the student's participation.

AMBASSADOR: What kind of music do you like?

STUDENT: [names contemporary band or song]

AMBASSADOR: I like that music, too. Let's play that and dance to it. Ready? Set? Go!

The Ambassador plays the music, but not terribly loud, and she and the student dance for approximately 30 seconds. Then the Ambassador hits the stop button and the music stops.

AMBASSADOR: You know what? That was so much fun I want to do it again!

STUDENT: Okay!

The Ambassador plays the music, louder this time, but not at eardrum-shattering volume.

The Ambassador is desensitizing the student to the loud noise by gradually turning up the volume. Should the student have an adverse reaction to the noise, the Ambassador should lower the volume, then keep raising it in smaller and smaller increments until the student no longer notices.

The Ambassador repeats this step until the music is at a level commensurate with that of most school dances.

AMBASSADOR: Great job dancing! But before we can be ready to go to the dance this Saturday, we have to do two things: play a game with the lights, and then practice our dance steps.

STUDENT: Why?

AMBASSADOR: Well, the light game is going to be pretty fun. But it's also going to be pretty dark in the dance, so we have to be really good at our dance moves so we don't bump into each other. Or anyone else. Okay?

STUDENT: Okay.

AMBASSADOR: Great. So do you want to play the lights game or be in control of the music?

STUDENT: Lights.

It doesn't matter which of the two the student chooses; the point is to get him accustomed to the environment. Additionally, many school dances involve physical games, and adding a more game-like component to the exercise is also good preparation for these games.

AMBASSADOR: Okay, ready? Go!

The student flips the lights on and off while the Ambassador blasts the music. After 30 seconds, the Ambassador stops the music.

AMBASSADOR: Okay, ready to dance?

STUDENT: Yes!

The student and Ambassador are joined by several other Ambassadors, two of whom control the lights and music.

AMBASSADOR: Okay, but one last thing: At a dance, you can just go out and dance, or you can ask someone to dance with you while the music is playing.

STUDENT: [nods]

This qualifies as gravy for this module; some students might have advanced enough social skills that they will feel comfortable asking another student to dance, but it is not necessary. The Ambassador should evaluate the student's level of sociability and decide whether or not to include this step accordingly.

AMBASSADOR: Okay—ready? Let's dance!

The other Ambassadors create a light and music show while the Ambassador, student, and other Ambassadors dance.

We have already mentioned that games are often played at dances; these are often conducted by the deejay. Some deejays make a point of talking loudly over the microphone in between, and even during, songs. Therefore, another optional step is to give a microphone to an Ambassador and have her bark out song titles, dance moves, et cetera, over the microphone.

AMBASSADOR: Great job! I can't wait for Saturday!

Outro

The goal of the module was to desensitize students with autism to the loud chaos of a school dance. Every stage was presented incrementally, with the music gradually getting louder as the light component was worked in so that it ultimately became an organic part of the dance. Additional potential distractions, like games, vocal deejays, and asking someone else to dance, were factored into the module as well. Ambassadors should also be aware whether the dance has any costume theme, or motif of any other sort, and work that into the action set forth in the module.

As with all other modules, it is imperative that Ambassadors anticipate distracting situations that might arise and use their training to refocus the student's attention back on the task at hand. If necessary, it is fine for the Ambassador to improvise, as long as the improvisation falls well within the range of acceptable behavior. Should more assistance be necessary, the Ambassador should not hesitate to engage a teacher or schoolyard supervisor.

SECTION 6

Sports Modules

We live in an age and a culture in which achievement on the athletic field has never been more important. For all the background noise about their importance in our culture, however, sports play a vital role both in terms of physical fitness and social acceptance. And for students with autism, achieving success in sports can be a shortcut to the latter. Witness the case of Jason McElwain, the student with autism who nailed six three-pointers late in a basketball game and became not only a hit in school but all over the Internet as well. Even for students without McElwain's proficiency, the athletic field can be a place of focus, of respite, an equalizer where a priority is placed on the principles of order and where everything makes sense.

Note that we have not provided comprehensive rulebooks and detailed strategies for the games and sports we are profiling; those would fill up a separate book. Our goal is simply to provide students and Ambassadors with some introductory teaching techniques through which the basic rules of, and approaches to, these activities can be explained logically and clearly.

The four modules that make up this section are as follows:

1. Playing Soccer
2. Playing Tag
3. Playing Football
4. Playing Tetherball

Playing Soccer addresses the sport that is the world's most popular, and has become, in the past generation, a virtual rite of passage for many of this country's youth. Soccer, even more than football, involves a cabal-like team at the center of its culture, the positive social ramifications of which go without saying. This module breaks soccer down into passing and dribbling and even makes a point of teaching the distinction between the word *soccer* and the international term, *football.*

Playing Tag addresses this playground game, which can create problems for students with autism. Because the entire game revolves around one student touching another—more often than not in a brusque, decidedly ungentle way—considerable challenges exist for the student with tactile issues. This module desensitizes the student with autism to the game so that she can enjoy the playground without feeling insecure.

Playing Football breaks down the basics of the sport that has enduringly been this country's most popular. NFL and college football are enjoying unprecedented levels of popularity, and even if the student has no interest in playing, he (or she—plenty of women love to discuss, and feel partial to, football teams) can earn significant social points simply by being conversant on the subject. This module teaches the essential components—running, passing, and receiving—of football using the flag method, as students with autism might have tactile issues that would make teaching touch (and especially tackle) football too difficult.

Playing Tetherball takes another popular playground game and uses repetition and basic step increments to teach this more-complicated-than-it-looks game to students with autism. The Ambassador teaches the student about the game's reversals and blocking techniques so that the student can approach typical students on the playground and join in, in accordance with our module **Finding Friends at Lunch**.

Playing Soccer

*An Autism Ambassadors
Original Module*

Intro

The purpose of this module is to teach students with autism how to play soccer, which has rapidly become one of this generation's preferred activities. Learning how to play soccer will allow students with autism to gain entree into everything from pickup games to organized American Youth Soccer Organization (AYSO) events, thus allowing them to fit in to more of their peers' activities. Because soccer is so internationally popular, this sport also offers students with autism an opportunity to break the ice socially in any country they might happen to be visiting.

For this module, we are going to incorporate elements of our modules **Playing Tag** and **Playing Football** to address first how to dribble, then how to pass, and then finally how to shoot the ball.

Since soccer, unlike games like tag, involves equipment that cannot be simulated, an actual ball and goal (it can be a small one of the sort that is used on smaller fields or in games played among younger children) will be required for the module. Ambassadors might also wish to teach the game in an indoor facility, such as a school gym, due to the potential for the ball to be difficult to control for students first learning how to play. We will require other students to role-play everything from the student with special needs to the other students in the play area. Student simulators will stand near the student with autism while the Ambassador will stand next to the student with autism.

As with all of our other modules, should the student show signs of extended disengagement or display self-stimulatory behavior with her hands, the Ambassador should refer to our introductory module **Pay Attention/Calm Hands** in order to get the student to be fully present for the lesson.

We are now ready to begin. The Ambassador leads the student with autism into the playground area, over to the soccer goal.

AMBASSADOR: (Student's name), I've got a great idea—let's play soccer!

> Because soccer is known as football in practically every other country in the world other than America, Ambassadors should substitute the word *football* for the word *soccer* as need be for international students.

STUDENT: [looks around the playground area; looks nervous]

AMBASSADOR: I love soccer. Do you?

STUDENT: [nods]

AMBASSADOR: Do you know how to play soccer?

STUDENT: [touches her foot, or does something else related to feet—kicks the ground, tap dances, etc.]

> Students with autism frequently respond with non sequiturs or give semirelevant responses. As with all of our other modules, Ambassadors should always be prepared to redirect the conversation back to the task at hand without giving the impression that the student has misunderstood.

AMBASSADOR: What are you doing?

STUDENT: Playing with my foot.

AMBASSADOR: That looks like fun, and maybe we can play something like that later. But right now I would really love to play soccer, which is like football because we use our feet for both sports. Do you know how to play soccer?

STUDENT: No.

> The student might say "yes" and might have watched a fair amount of soccer, but that is far different from knowing how to physically play the game.

AMBASSADOR: No problem. Soccer is a really easy game to learn that is also lots of fun. Here, let me show you.

AMBASSADOR: [drops the ball on the ground] In soccer, you want to move the ball up the field and try to kick it into the goal. A player called the goalie will try to block you from scoring. If you can kick it in, or pass to another one of your teammates who kicks it in, your team gets a goal. The team with the most goals at the end of the game wins.

Depending on how high functioning the student is, the Ambassador can break down the above instructions into a series of one-step prompts. In addition, the Ambassador should consider using a whiteboard and markers, similar to what actual coaches use, should he want to diagram basic moves.

AMBASSADOR: [demonstrating basic dribbling moves] In soccer you can't use your hands unless you're guarding the goal. You can only use your feet to move the ball up the field. It's called *dribbling*.

The ideal Ambassador should be experienced in soccer but not so flashy that his ball-handling skills overwhelm or intimidate the student.

AMBASSADOR: Let's say I want to move the ball upfield fast, or let's say I'm being guarded closely by a player from the other team. So I decide that I'm going to pass the ball to you.

The Ambassador passes the ball to the student.

AMBASSADOR: Your turn. Dribble the ball.

The student kicks the ball hard, but the Ambassador stops it.

The Ambassador should be ready for the ball to careen all over the playground and should be prepared to chase the ball; a confined area and/or more Ambassadors to act as a de facto backstop can be helpful.

AMBASSADOR: Okay, that was a nice start, but let's try dribbling the ball. Why don't you start by dribbling the ball over to me? Just like I did it. Here, let me show you again.

The Ambassador dribbles the ball over to the student.

AMBASSADOR: Dribble the ball over to me.

STUDENT: [dribbles the ball]

AMBASSADOR: Great dribbling! Now let me show you how to pass the ball.

The Ambassador repeats the steps above for passing and shooting. When it comes time to teach shooting, another Ambassador should play goalie; should another Ambassador not be available, the first Ambassador should first pass the ball to the student, then play goalie.

AMBASSADOR: Great passing and shooting! Now let's play with some of the other kids!

> If the student still seems nervous or shy about playing with another kid, refer to the module **Finding Friends at Lunch,** in which we address teaching students with autism to identify friendly faces in the crowd and join them.

The Ambassador and student with autism join the game and play with the other kids in the playground area.

Outro

The objective of this module was to teach students with autism how to play soccer and integrate themselves into the playground activity. For this module, we taught Ambassadors how to assuage any anxiety on the part of the student while positively reinforcing the student's progress. Because soccer, like football, involves numerous skill sets—dribbling, passing, shooting, and goaltending—the steps above should be repeated for as long as a student wishes, in order to learn all facets of the game.

As with all other modules, it is imperative that Ambassadors anticipate distracting situations that might arise and use their training to refocus the student's attention back on the task at hand. If necessary, it is fine for the Ambassador to improvise, as long as the improvisation falls well within the range of acceptable behavior. Should more assistance be necessary, the Ambassador should not hesitate to engage a teacher or schoolyard supervisor.

Playing Tag

An Autism Ambassadors
Original Module

Intro

The purpose of this module is to teach students with autism, especially younger ones, how to play the popular recess and lunchtime game of tag. Recess is a necessary respite from class activities that every student needs and should look forward to, but games of tag and the like are frequently viewed by students with autism as chaotic and disorienting; more often than not, these students tend to tune out and become more anxious than they typically are. The goal is to get students with autism to participate in and enjoy the game of tag, thus enabling them to blend in with, and subsequently be better accepted by, their classmates while also enjoying some physical activity.

The module will simulate a lunch area setting. A tape recorder or CD player will be present to provide background noise. We will require other students to role-play everything from the student with autism to the other students in the play area. The student simulators will sit at seats near the student with autism, while the Ambassador will sit in a seat next to the student with autism.

As with all of our other modules, should the student show signs of extended disengagement or display self-stimulatory behavior with her hands, the Ambassador should refer to our introductory module **Pay Attention/Calm Hands** in order to get the student to be fully present for the module.

We are now ready to begin. The Ambassador leads the student into the playground area.

AMBASSADOR: (Student's name), it's recess. Time to play our favorite games!

STUDENT: [looks around the playground area; looks nervous]

AMBASSADOR: [points to some kids playing tag] Hmm, looks like those kids are playing tag! That's one of my favorite games!

> Repetition of the word *favorite* can help to discourage any trepidation on the part of the student with autism. As with many of our other modules, Ambassadors should proudly share their love of, and enthusiasm for, the activities in which they are about to participate.

STUDENT: [looks down at hands and darts eyes around, muttering under her breath]

AMBASSADOR: Do you know how to play tag?

STUDENT: [touches her foot, or does something else related to feet—kicks the ground, tap dances, etc.]

> Students with autism frequently respond with non sequiturs or give semirelevant responses. As with all of our other modules, Ambassadors should always be prepared to redirect the conversation back to the task at hand without giving the impression that the student has misunderstood.

AMBASSADOR: What are you doing?

STUDENT: Tapping my foot.

AMBASSADOR: That looks like fun, and maybe we can play something like that later. But right now I would really love to play tag. Do you know how to play?

STUDENT: No.

AMBASSADOR: Do you want me to show you how to play?

STUDENT: [flaps hands]

AMBASSADOR: There's nothing to be worried about. It's a really fun game, and it's easy to learn. All you have to do is run around, wherever you want, and try not to get touched on the shoulder by the person who is "it." That means you are tagged, and it is your turn to be "it."

STUDENT: I don't like to be touched.

AMBASSADOR: I don't like it either, but it's really quick and it's over fast, and then you get to be the one to touch the other person. Would you like to try?

STUDENT: Okay.

AMBASSADOR: First I'll be "it," which means I'll try to tag you first with my hand.

The Ambassador chases the student with autism around until he tags the student.

AMBASSADOR: I tagged you! Now you're it! That means it's your turn to try to tag me!

STUDENT: [starts to throw a tantrum]

It is important to remember that many students with autism have sensory issues and might be sensitive to someone else touching them, so the Ambassador should make sure that the tag itself on the student's body is not applied too hard. Even if the tag is not applied too hard, it is still possible that the student will become alarmed by the sensation of being touched and will react. Ambassadors should be prepared for a tantrum, as well as any other type of setback reflective of fear or anxiety on the part of the student.

AMBASSADOR: You're doing great in this game! I just tagged you; don't be upset. Everyone gets tagged, and everyone gets to tag other people back. That's why the game is so fun; because everyone gets to be equal. Now it's your turn to tag me!

The Ambassador should not only reiterate the rules of the game, as repetition is a key to all lesson plans pertaining to students with autism, but should also emphasize the fact that tagging doesn't make a student stand out in any way; it's all part of the fun of the game. This will help alleviate any anxiety a student with autism might have that she is being stigmatized or picked on.

STUDENT: Why do you want me to tag you?

AMBASSADOR: I don't want you to tag me; I want you to try your best to tag me so you won't be "it" anymore—I'll be "it," and you can go back to running around and trying not to be tagged!

The student chases the Ambassador around the playground.

When it is the turn of the student with autism to be it, the Ambassador shouldn't try too hard not to be tagged but also shouldn't make it look as though he isn't trying at all.

AMBASSADOR: [gets tagged by student] Oh, you tagged me! Say, "you're it"!

STUDENT: You're it!

AMBASSADOR: Great playing tag! Now let's go play tag with a group of other kids!

In addition to frequently repeating the name of the activity, it is always a good idea for Ambassadors to compliment the student with autism whenever she completes any part of the activity successfully.

> If the student with autism still seems nervous or shy about joining the other kids, refer to the module **Finding Friends at Lunch,** in which we address teaching students with autism to identify friendly faces in the crowd and join them.

The Ambassador and student with autism join the game and play with the other kids in the playground area.

Outro

The objective of this module was to teach students with autism how to play tag and integrate themselves into the playground activity. For this module, we taught Ambassadors how to assuage any anxiety on the part of the student with autism while positively reinforcing the student's progress. The physical aspects of the game were incorporated into it without ignoring any potential tactile sensitivity on the part of the student with autism, and the Ambassador was given a number of options he could employ should the student have an adverse reaction to the game.

As with all other modules, it is imperative that Ambassadors anticipate distracting situations that might arise and use their training to refocus the student's attention back on the task at hand. If necessary, it is fine for the Ambassador to improvise, as long as the improvisation falls well within the range of acceptable behavior. Should more assistance be necessary, the Ambassador should not hesitate to engage a teacher or schoolyard supervisor.

Playing Football

*An Autism Ambassadors
Original Module*

Intro

The purpose of this module is to teach students with autism how to play football, which is currently America's most-watched sport and is only growing in popularity each year. Teaching students with autism how to play will, by extension, teach them how to appreciate watching and commenting on the sport, which will only help the students achieve their goal of fitting in with their peers even more.

For this module, we are going to incorporate elements of our modules **Playing Tag** and **Playing Soccer** to break down the essential steps of the game: First we will teach students how to throw the ball; then we will teach them how to run with it. And because many students with autism have tactile issues and are sensitive to anything that involves physical contact, we will use rip-off waistband flags of the variety used in flag football leagues and will not teach tag or tackle football.

Since football, like soccer, involves equipment that cannot be simulated, an actual ball and actual waistband flags will be required for the module. We will require other students to role-play everything from the student with special needs to the other students in the play area. Student simulators will stand near the student with autism, while the Ambassador will stand next to the student with autism.

As with all of our other modules, should the student show signs of extended disengagement or display self-stimulatory behavior with his hands, the Ambassador should refer to our introductory module **Pay Attention/Calm Hands** in order to get the student to be fully present for the lesson.

We are now ready to begin. The Ambassador leads the student with autism into the playground area.

AMBASSADOR: (Student's name), I've got a great idea—let's play football!

STUDENT: [looks around the playground area; looks nervous]

> Because *football* is the word commonly used for soccer internationally, Ambassadors should make sure that, if working with students from an international background, they are clear that they will be playing American football.

AMBASSADOR: I love football; do you?

STUDENT: [nods]

AMBASSADOR: Do you know how to play football?

STUDENT: [touches his foot, or does something else related to feet— kicks the ground, tap dances, etc.]

> Students with autism frequently respond with non sequiturs or give semirelevant responses. As with all of our other modules, Ambassadors should always be prepared to redirect the conversation back to the task at hand without giving the impression that the student has misunderstood.

AMBASSADOR: What are you doing?

STUDENT: I'm playing with my feet.

AMBASSADOR: That looks like fun, and maybe we can play that later. But right now I would really love to play football. Do you know how to play?

STUDENT: No.

AMBASSADOR: No problem. It's really easy to learn and lots of fun.

The Ambassador wraps flags around both his waist and the student's waist.

AMBASSADOR: First we have to put on our flags. A flag is something you rip off other players to stop them from scoring. It's like playing tag.

> The Ambassador should refer to the module **Playing Tag**, which will help the student with autism understand the concept of being tagged and becoming "it," which in football is the same idea as the play being whistled dead.

AMBASSADOR: First I'm going to teach you how to play. There are two teams. One team has the ball and is trying to move the ball into the other team's goal. That's called an end zone, and when they move the ball into the end zone, that's called a touchdown. Say "touchdown."

STUDENT: Touchdown.

AMBASSADOR: All right! So you can make a touchdown by running with the ball into the end zone, or by throwing the ball to another player and having him run with the ball into the end zone.

> The Ambassador should feel free to diagram the finer points of football scoring on a whiteboard or piece of paper, much in the same way a football coach would.

AMBASSADOR: Now that's what the team on offense does. The team on defense tries to stop the team on offense. The way they stop the team on offense is by ripping the flag off of the person with the ball. You want me to show you how?

STUDENT: Yes.

AMBASSADOR: Okay. I'm going to run toward the end zone. You rip off my flag.

The Ambassador runs—not too quickly—toward the end zone, and the student rips the flag off his belt.

AMBASSADOR: That was great! Now let's do it the other way around: I want you to run toward the end zone and try not to get caught by me.

The Ambassador hands the ball to the student, who runs around in circles.

AMBASSADOR: That was great running, but let's try running only toward the end zone. And you can't run out of bounds.

> The student might need to be redirected several times, as football is more like soccer and less like tag in this regard; the Ambassador needs to remind the student that he is only to run in the direction that his team is facing. Please refer to our modules **Playing Soccer** for rules about the field's boundaries, and **Playing Tag** for additional tips on overall principles involving tactile games.

AMBASSADOR: Great running! Now let's try a pass play! It's the same as a running play, only first you run without the football toward the end zone, and then when I say to turn around, I want you to turn around and I'll throw the ball to you. Then I want you run to the end zone and try not to get caught by the other players.

> Depending on how high functioning the student is, the above steps can be broken down into three single-step prompts, instead of the three-step prompt above.

STUDENT: [runs about five yards]

AMBASSADOR: Turn around!

STUDENT: [continues running toward the end zone and turns around when in it]

AMBASSADOR: (Student's name), that's one kind of way to score a touchdown, but you have to be holding the ball. So let's try it again, but this time I want you to run while counting to five, and then turn around.

> Counting is an extremely effective tool when working with students with autism. In this situation, we are using a five-count not to calm the student down, but to give him a prompt of a different kind, namely, when to turn around to catch the ball.

The student runs five yards, counting to five, and then turns around, and the Ambassador throws the ball to him.

AMBASSADOR: Great catch! Now run to the end zone!

STUDENT: [runs to the end zone]

AMBASSADOR: Great job! Now let's play a game of football with some of the other kids!

> If the student still seems nervous or shy about playing with other students, refer to the module **Finding Friends at Lunch,** in which we teach students how to identify friendly faces in the crowd and join them.

The Ambassador and student with autism join the game and play with the other kids in the playground area.

Outro

The objective of this module was to teach students with autism how to play football and integrate themselves into the playground activity. Because football is such a complicated game, the Ambassador should use the approaches outlined above to teach key ingredients of defense and kicking the ball as well.

Additionally, students should be taught that blocking is a key part of the game, and should have the more physical ingredients of the game taught to them using the same step-by-step process outlined in the module above. Note that because of the previously mentioned tactile issues, blocking might be a significant hurdle for these students to overcome; the Ambassador should gauge her student accordingly, and, if the student simply cannot be counted on to block, should give the student only throwing, running, and receiving duties.

As with all other modules, it is imperative that Ambassadors anticipate distracting situations that might arise and use their training to refocus the student's attention back on the task at hand. If necessary, it is fine for the Ambassador to improvise, as long as the improvisation falls well within the range of acceptable behavior. Should more assistance be necessary, the Ambassador should not hesitate to engage a teacher or schoolyard supervisor.

Playing Tetherball

*An Autism Ambassadors
Original Module*

Intro

The purpose of this module is to teach students with autism, especially younger ones, how to play the popular and enduring game of tetherball, a playground game that is relatively simple but has the potential to be physically daunting and harmful to a student with autism. For this module, we are going to incorporate elements of our modules **Playing Tag** and **Finding A Friend at Lunch** to address first how to teach the elements of the game and second how to find someone with whom to play it.

Since tetherball, unlike tag, involves an apparatus that cannot be simulated, an actual tetherball pole and ball will be required for the module. We will require other students to role-play everything from the student with autism to the other students in the play area. The student simulators will sit at seats near the student with autism, while the Ambassador will sit in a seat next to the student with autism.

As with all of our other modules, should the student show signs of extended disengagement or display self-stimulatory behavior with her hands, the Ambassador should refer to our introductory module **Pay Attention/Calm Hands** in order to get the student to be fully present for the module.

We are now ready to begin. The Ambassador leads the student with autism into the playground area and over to the tetherball pole, and positions the two of them on opposite sides of the pole.

AMBASSADOR: (Student's name), it's recess. Do you like tetherball?

STUDENT: [looks around the playground area; looks nervous]

AMBASSADOR: I love tetherball. I've been playing it since I was little, and I'd love someone to play with.

> Ambassadors are role models for students with autism. Even if they are not natural enthusiasts of the game or activity, they should, as with all other activities, always stress their love of, and history enjoying, the activity at hand.

AMBASSADOR: Do you know how to play tetherball?

STUDENT: Yes.

AMBASSADOR: Would you like to teach me how to play tetherball?

STUDENT: Yes.

STUDENT: [grabs the pole and runs around it in circles]

> Students with autism frequently respond with non sequiturs or give semi-relevant responses. As with all of our other modules, Ambassadors should always be prepared to redirect the conversation back to the task at hand without giving the impression that the student has misunderstood.

AMBASSADOR: That looks like fun, and maybe we can play that game you're playing later on. But right now I would really love to play tetherball. Do you know how to play tetherball?

STUDENT: No.

AMBASSADOR: [picks up the tetherball] Let me show you how to play. What you want to do is stand on the other side of the pole and block the ball from going around when I throw it.

STUDENT: Why?

AMBASSADOR: Because then the ball will come all the way around the pole again to me and you won't get a chance to throw it. If you want a chance to throw it, you need to stop it before it gets past you, and to do that, you block it with your hands.

STUDENT: Okay.

The Ambassador throws the ball, but the student just watches as the ball makes a full circle around the pole.

AMBASSADOR: Okay, let's try again: I'll throw the ball and you block it this time.

The Ambassador throws the ball, and this time the student blocks it.

AMBASSADOR: Great block! Now throw it toward me!

The student throws the ball, but the wrong way. The ball continues around the pole and winds up back in the Ambassador's hand.

AMBASSADOR: That was a great try, but you want to throw the ball toward me so I can try to block it.

STUDENT: [holds the ball and flaps for a moment]

Many students with autism stim, or exhibit self-stimulatory behavior, that involves their hands. The Ambassador should always attempt to redirect the student's hands toward the activity in which they are participating, and tetherball offers an excellent opportunity to do so.

AMBASSADOR: Why don't you throw the ball and I'll try to block it?

As is the case in many of our other modules, Ambassadors should repeat prompts that are not followed.

The student throws the ball and the Ambassador blocks it.

AMBASSADOR: Great job! Now it's my turn to throw and your turn to block!

The Ambassador throws the ball, and this time the student blocks it.

AMBASSADOR: Great block!

The Ambassador should both demonstrate the proper defensive technique and compliment the student for copying that technique.

AMBASSADOR: Now you throw the ball and try to get it past my block.

The student throws the ball, and the Ambassador lets it go past his block. The ball circles around the pole.

AMBASSADOR: Great job! Now hit the ball again so it goes past my block again.

The student hits the ball again, and again it goes past the Ambassador's block.

AMBASSADOR: Great job! Now keep hitting the ball until it goes all the way around the pole!

The Ambassador should not only continue to compliment the student, but should also emphasize the need to follow the game through to completion.

AMBASSADOR: Great job! Now let's start over and play a full game together!

The Ambassador and student with autism play tetherball.

While the Ambassador should by no means take it easy on the student with autism, the Ambassador should still inspire confidence by allowing the student with autism to block and score several wraps around the pole whenever possible.

AMBASSADOR: Great job playing tetherball with me! Now let's play a game of tetherball with another kid!

> If the student with autism still seems nervous or shy about playing with another kid, refer to the module **Finding Friends at Lunch,** in which we address teaching students with autism to identify friendly faces in the crowd and join them.

The Ambassador and student with autism play with the other kids in the playground area.

Outro

The objective of this module was to teach students with autism how to play tetherball and integrate themselves into the playground activity. We broke the game down into its essential components and taught Ambassadors how to assuage any anxiety on the part of the student while positively reinforcing the student's progress.

As with all other modules, it is imperative that Ambassadors anticipate distracting situations that might arise and use their training to refocus the student's attention back on the task at hand. If necessary, it is fine for the Ambassador to improvise, as long as the improvisation falls well within the range of acceptable behavior. Should more assistance be necessary, the Ambassador should not hesitate to engage a teacher or schoolyard supervisor.

PART III

Resources for Autism Ambassadors Clubs

RESOURCE A
Parent Letter

Hi Parents,

My name is Zak Kukoff, and I'm the 18-year-old founder of Autism Ambassadors (www.autismambassadors.org), a new peer-leadership program being offered at your school. Autism Ambassadors teaches students at your school how to teach students with autism social, emotional, and academic skills, and also helps to build friendships between typical students and those with special needs. The Autism Ambassadors program includes a curriculum component—developed and written by students and vetted by psychologists—that is offered at no cost to schools and meets the standards of the National Autism Center as an evidenced-based approach for working with students with autism.

Regardless of whether your child is typical or has special needs, the Autism Ambassadors program offers your child an opportunity to befriend and bond with other students. As part of the Ambassadors program, your child will help build a better environment for all children in the school.

What can Autism Ambassadors offer your child? If you're the parent of a child with special needs—regardless of whether your child has been diagnosed with autism—Autism Ambassadors offers the opportunity for your child to build a solid friend group and to learn vital social, emotional, and academic skills from peers. If you're the parent of a typical child, Autism Ambassadors offers a chance for your student to build vital leadership skills and friendships that will last a lifetime. Autism Ambassadors also offers your child the opportunity to significantly improve the quality of life for another student.

Autism Ambassadors has been successfully implemented in over 25 schools—from Alaska to Australia—and also works extensively with the Ventura County SELPA, the Special Education Localized Plan Area.

If you have any questions about Autism Ambassadors or would like to support our organization, please visit our website at autismambassadors.org, or e-mail me at zak@autismambassadors.org.

Thanks, and I look forward to hearing from you.

Zak Kukoff

Founder, Autism Ambassadors

zak@autismambassadors.org

RESOURCE B
Autism Ambassadors— Frequently Asked Questions

? Question—What is Autism Ambassadors?

Answer—Autism Ambassadors is a dynamic peer-leadership organization that is dedicated to building organic friendships between students with autism and typical students. The typical students (also called Ambassadors) use our curriculum not only to foster sustainable friendships (i.e., ones based on common interests and activities) but also to teach the students with autism social, emotional, and academic skills.

? Question—What is the Autism Ambassadors curriculum? How does it work?

Answer—The Autism Ambassadors curriculum is a series of lessons in module format that cover many aspects of a special needs student's day. Each module focuses on a few tasks and fully breaks them down and reinforces them, using role-playing and repetition, our "special sauce" based on the science of applied behavioral analysis.

? Question—Why role-playing? Isn't that for children?

Answer—We use role-playing because it is one of the most natural forms of communication, second only to talking. Role-playing, from a young age, is a skill that almost all typically developing children utilize daily. Examples include playing doctor, nurse, school, cops and robbers, or war. We use role-playing to instill a sense of empathy in the Ambassadors and teach them how to overcome their discomfort with students with autism. And yes, role-playing is for kids, but that's why we use it.

? Question—Is there a cost for the schools to implement this program?

Answer—No, Autism Ambassadors is fully funded and backed by angel investors and corporate donations. We provide our curriculum and training services as a no-cost program to any interested party.

? Question—What are the qualities of an Ambassador?

Answer—Ideally, Ambassadors should be hard-working, good students, responsible, and love helping others. They should be dedicated to their work, and a history of community service is a plus, albeit not a necessity. Ambassadors need to be strong enough students to be able to miss 30 to 45 minutes of class a week.

? Question—What does a school need to do to implement the curriculum?

Answer—Almost nothing. If a school finds a group of students (both Ambassadors and students with autism), we'll do the rest. Alternatively, students can start an Autism Ambassadors group, which requires only a faculty advisor.

? Question—How do we know if the Autism Ambassadors curriculum is working?

Answer—Autism Ambassadors provides an evaluation tool, developed by Zak Kukoff, the executive student advisory board, and numerous students with autism, that we administer to both the Ambassadors and students with autism at the beginning of the program and again at three-month intervals. We can use the results of this test to determine what, if any, changes need to be applied to the implementation at the specific school.

? Question—How can I find out more about Autism Ambassadors?

Answer—You can go to our website, www.autismambassadors.org, our Twitter site, www.twitter.com/auambassadors, our Facebook page, www.tr.im/ambass.

Personality Questionnaire

1) Are you a generally patient person?

   a. Yes   b. No   c. Sometimes

2) What are your hobbies?

3) Have you ever worked with students with autism?

   a. Yes   b. No

If yes, please explain:

4) Do you prefer a male or female student partner for the program?

   a. Male   b. Female

5) How often would you be able to help out a student with autism?

   a. All the time   b. Just at school   c. Only after school

6) Are there certain days when you cannot help your student? If so, please explain.

7) How did you find out about the Autism Ambassadors program?

     a. Through a friend   b. Through school   c. Through the media
     d. Through a parent   e. Other

Explain:

8) What extracurricular activities do you participate in?

9) What kind of student are you?

     a. Excellent   b. Good   c. Average   d. Poor

10) Have you worked with students with any other kind of special needs?

     a. Yes   b. No

RESOURCE D
Evaluation Questionnaire

We hope you are enjoying your experience as an Autism Ambassador so far! At this point in being an Ambassador, we ask you to fill in the following evaluation protocol. There is no limit to the length of your responses for this evaluation sheet. Please use as much room as you need, and feel free to continue on the back or on separate sheets of paper.

1. Describe the connection that you share with your counterpart with special needs.

2. Has the connection between you and the student grown or lessened? Please explain.

3. On a scale of 1 to 10, how much fun do you think that you and the student are having together?

   1   2   3   4   5   6   7   8   9   10

4. Do you feel as though the student has made significant progress through his or her time spent with you? How so?

5. In what ways have you changed as a person through the experience of being an Ambassador?

6. In what ways have you seen the student improve by using the Autism Ambassadors curriculum? (socially, mentally, etc.)

7. Do you have any suggestions regarding the Autism Ambassadors curriculum?

8. Do you have any suggestions for changes in the activities that we incorporate into our curriculum?

9. Would you consider recommending Autism Ambassadors to any friends? Why?

10. Describe the high and low points in your relationship with your counterpart with special needs.

References

Autism Speaks. (2012a, April 2). *Autism's costs to the nation reach $137 billion a year.* Retrieved from http://www.autismspeaks.org/science/science-news/autism%E2%80%99s-costs-nation-reach-137-billion-year

Autism Speaks. (2012b, March 30). *Media coverage of 1 in 88 autism prevalence numbers.* Retrieved from http://www.autismspeaks.org/blog/2012/03/30/media-coverage-1-88-autism-prevalence-numbers

Laushey, K. M., & Heflin, J. (2000). Enhancing social skills of kindergarten children with autism through the training of multiple peers as tutors. *Journal of Autism and Developmental Disorders, 30*(3), 183–193.

Sandler, M. (2012). *Football heroes: Making a difference—Troy Polamalu.* New York, NY: Bearport.

Index